Wow, wow, wow, I could not put this book down. Honest, Deep, emotional, liberating. Beautifully written, you will not be able to help but feel moved by Anna's words and story. Anna has an amazing ability to help you look within yourself, to unfold what you need to and lovingly repack so you can move forward with your travels in this beautiful life.

Such an honour and a pleasure to read.
Naomi Borbasi Nurse, HH.Dip (C)

"When Life Comes Along....I found it raw, confronting, and vulnerable. It challenged every aspect of my life, mortality (currently fighting metastatic cancer), honesty (mine and others) strength, courage, kindness, and compassion. It held me accountable in the most honest compassionate way. It awakened my need to hold myself to higher standards, to believe in myself, to never give up, and to honour the life I have been entrusted as caretaker of.

Thank you, Anna, for your vulnerability, for sharing your pain, your wisdom and your journey so that we too can heal."

Your book is amazing Anna, I cried like a baby, I visited my own mortality in very real time. It gave me the courage to have difficult conversations around death with my kids. The way in which you hold us accountable for who we are, the decisions/ choices we make is done with kindness and compassion......I will read it again, and again......I put a shelf in my campervan today just for your books lol...... they will be my companions.

Sharon Heath
Dip Paramedicine, Cancer warrior and proud mum of three beautiful young adults.

Anna Hamilton is a woman of many talents, a successful author, Relationship coach, Women's Health and myofascial specialist, senior yoga teacher and has written her third book titled "When Life Comes Along."

In this book, Anna delves deep into the human psyche, below the surface of the everyday life, beyond the hard times, the struggles, the doubts, the insecurities, hurts, grief, and disappointments we all experience, and invites, no URGES the reader to confront, ignite or maybe reignite the unrealised dreams, the self-confidence they may have once had, to be honest, to reflect and move towards becoming the person they dream to be, to live the life they really want and deserve. She raises the questions we have been too afraid, exhausted, anxious, or fearful to ask or to face. She puts the power firmly back into the readers hands, life is fragile, our time on this planet brief, is this how you want to live? YOU have choice.

This book will make you cry, laugh, confront your own fears, and question your reactions, feelings, and beliefs. It will open your eyes, to possibilities, dare you to be brave and step out of your comfort zone.

The passion and knowledge Anna has shines through in her writing, her own personal stories, her emotive poetry, her understanding of the physiology of the body and the spiritual connection to self, nature, the universe. She acknowledges that we are human, with many and varied facets to our personalities, we have strengths and weaknesses, and that every experience good and bad is an opportunity for growth but it's up to us what we choose to do.

A few words and paragraphs do not do justice to this book.

It is a powerful read, and if you were to only read one book for the year then this should be the one you choose.

Congratulations Anna!
Kaylene Foote
Retired educator

Takes Courage…. to Change….and to read this book!

I took a deep breath, knowing some of these pages were not going to be easy, since it never is 'When Life Comes Along.' My heart ached; and my soul filled with a kind of dis-ease that can only be felt when another bares their inner most secrets. This heartfelt saga reveals how paralyzing afflictions could be transformed into fuel-for-healing and Anna shows us how.

In this third self-healing trilogy, Anna is again our trusted guide for navigating the darkest crevices of our soul-journey. Our trusted teacher, has so bravely shared her darkest moments so that we might face ours.

Page after page, I was taken into the darkest depths of Anna's soul, then lifted-up in thoughtful reverence by her beautiful poetry. I was shown how to take stock, move through and move on from my own trauma. My perspective has been shifted (again), from fearful to fearless, victim to warrior and sick person to healer of self. The journey to answer the relentless question, 'who am I?' was birthed into knowing who, 'I am.' We are shown how to heal the whole self.

This healing journey is difficult but enroute we will drop off our victim-self and pick-up our warrior, the one who remains in the light despite the darkness, and who will help us move through and on from our own trauma.

Anna shares her most intimate losses and tragedies, as though the reader is her best friend, sharing her scattered ashes so that we may 'befriend our mind' and replace that relentless question, 'who am I?' with 'I am.' A priceless gift!

We are shown how discovering triumph out of tragedy comes from being disciplined and how our scattered ashes can be used to lay the foundation for our freedom. We simply must accept the challenge to 'uncover the cover-up.' Let's begin!

Paula Curtis
Functional Medicine Certified Coach, Holistic Medicine for Addiction Certified, Sweet Liberty Coaching, Owner

I am overwhelmed by this book of such beauty, poetry, and profundity. Anna takes you by the hand and with grace guides you through "When Life Comes Along", with heart, kindness and understanding.

I have been moved to tears by Anna's honesty, observation, and emotion. It takes courage to share our lives in such a personal way and Anna does so in an authentic voice.

With infinite care and personal experience, we are led on a path to healing. The wisdom, we as readers will gain on our journey of listening and learning, hoping, and hearing is permission giving, to live our own authentic life.

Join Anna as she gently encourages you to be pulled into the now, because that is all there is. Learn to recognise grace, feel forgiveness, and experience peace. Relinquish the rage and find release in these pages, as your heart relaxes.

To read this book is a gift. Anna's gift.

Rosemerrie Wright
Health Professional and Educator

This beautifully crafted book delivers a profound and honest message about life, consciousness, and human potential. Anna invites us to reflect deeply on the unfolding journey of existence, reminding us that life is precious and time moves forward – whether we embrace it or simply watch it pass.

She challenges us to examine the narratives that shape our lives:

- Are we truly living?
- Do we recognize the fleeting nature of time?
- Can we forgive others?
- Can we forgive ourselves?

Anna creates a safe and sacred space to explore life's deepest questions, guiding us toward a greater understanding of purpose, peace and self-awareness. She encourages us to pause with wisdom, to revisit past choices, and to uncover their impact on our journey.

She if **BRAVE**. She is **BOLD**. She speaks her **TRUTH.**

Through the courage of her personal storytelling, Anna forges a connection between her experiences and the reader's own life path she shares openly, inviting us to embrace our own wounds, triumphs, and transformations.

Anna, thank you for reminding us that life is not something that happens to us- it is something we create. The power to shape it, to live with intention, to embrace joy, and to rise through challenges has always been within us.

Rani Harlow Intuitive Guidance Counsellor

Oh wow, what can I say? So as always, I found myself not able to sleep, so I got up at 5.30 am this morning and stared reading your book. I am not a morning person, and over two hours later I am still reading. I can't put it down. Through the smiles and tears, I am looking at life in a different way, and, have learned so much about myself already. This is truly going to help so many people.

I moved through so many emotions while reading this book. One minute I was laughing, the next, I was in tears. This book will be my go-to when I feel life is overwhelming or I feel stressed, and doubt myself. It gave me comfort. This book has encouraged me to relax more into life, forgive myself and live more not only in the now, but also for the future.

Robynn Dental Assistant, Mum, and part time carer for a loved one with Alzheimer's.

"When Life Comes Along" is an inspirational guide to transformation, to living with a conscious awareness, reflecting, listening to yourself and others, healing, connecting with the divine, making a commitment to yourself, and as Anna says, 'to make a difference' and 'shine bright'.

Anna's writing is engaging, prompting readers to reflect on life from birth to death and consider, "What are you doing with your time?" Each chapter invites thoughtful reflection, urging the reader to truly listen to their body, mind, and spirit.

Anna bravely shares her personal healing journey, encouraging the reader to reflect on their own life and gain a deeper understanding of themselves. She encourages the reader to explore, to listen, to heal, to be disciplined, and to live life fully.

Anna is an inspiring teacher who embodies wellness, throughout the book she shares numerous daily practices, disciplines, and her deep connections with nature.

The book is amazing, engaging and beautifully written; I didn't want to put it down and can't wait to read it again.

Colleen Morgan.
Natural Therapist, Bachelor of Complementary Medicine, Melbourne Australia.

Anna takes us on a personal journey through life's challenges and shows us, that when life happens, we can embrace these challenges as opportunities to grow and evolve.

A delightful blend of poetry and personal revelations, that explore how our deepest wounds can become our greatest teachers. Anna skillfully inspires us to become the version of ourselves that has been hidden beneath layers of doubt fear and unresolved grief and trauma.

Congratulations on such a well written engaging, poetic, honest and revealing story to inspire, motivate and on which to contemplate,

A really good read and hard to put down!

Louise Wiggins
Yoga to Health Seaford

Anna Hamilton in her latest book "When Life Comes Along" gives the reader a deep and rare insight into her unique experiences, life, death and many things in between. She articulates the mind body connection, illness, pain, grief and loss alongside the highs of acceptance, love and hope. The author encourages us to lean into life's pain and discomfort and shed the ideas of 'victim' to embrace and make room for growth. She invites us to become our own leader, listen and be embodied and to trust and be curious about the challenges that we face or have faced. Anna gives us a pathway to understand the true freedom of self - an acceptance and commitment to practices of the mind and body that build a strength within us for now and into the future.

Thank you, Anna, for taking me deeper into my mind processes and how these relate to my day-to-day thoughts and actions. This book is profound and gives the reader more power over their unconscious processes and the tools to create a life that has intention and peace.

Trisha Higgins – Accredited Mental Health Social Worker

A remarkable book encompassing truly important facets of life.

Anna guides us to empower our own journey, honour feelings and inner voice, discover a strong sense of self and meaning to build confidence towards a new path forward.

A self-healing guide to maintain mental health, dealing with depression and depressive disorders. Giving hope when we think there is no answer.

Di - Nurse Australia

Table of Contents

When Life Comes Along

What will you do?

What can you overcome?

And who will you become?

BY ANNA HAMILTON

The author of this book does not dispense medical advice or prescribe the use of any technique as a form of treatment for physical, emotional or medical problems without the advice of a qualified physician.
The intent of the author is to share and offer information to help you on your quest for a more spiritual and authentic life. Therefore enhancing your wellbeing in all areas of your life.

Thankyou

Anna xxx

ISBN: 978-0-6480308-4-3

Anna's other books

Rising with the Phoenix
Heal the Whole Woman

I dedicate this book to Joshua and Hunter.
I hope, as your Mum, I have shared with you,
just as my parents shared with me, the little
life 'bytes' of wisdom to draw upon when you need it ....
when life comes along.

Anna, while having had a wonderful, loving childhood, also had a childhood which ran alongside her blissful one.

One in which forced her to either sink or swim. She eventually chose to swim.

She started practicing yoga at age 18, which became a solid foundation, even in times when things crumbled around her.

She has experienced trauma on many levels, loss of innocence, loss of loved ones, loss of self, eating disorders, type A personality, perfectionist, abusive, addictive behaviours, suicidal tendencies, poor body image, her own worst enemy.

All of which, she now draws upon to inspire others to go from living in their pain/ suffering body and mind, and turning their wounds into assets.

Anna is a hairdresser by trade, she studied yoga and became a qualified senior teacher and teacher trainer. This then led into becoming a remedial therapist and myofascial therapist, including trigger point therapy and energy work. She also specializes in pelvic floor health, incontinence and prolapse.

She has ridden horses nearly all her life, walks or runs most days, practices yoga, rides her push bike, loves being on the back of a motorbike with her husband, she is married to the love of her life for 27 years, a very proud Mum of two beautiful young men, she is still a farm girl at heart, and happiest with her fingers in the dirt.

Anna is happiest walking or sitting on a beach, and most definitely being in the ocean, she honours her cravings as frequently as she can to hike the snowy mountains, and she has recently discovered a deep love for the desert.

She is a recluse by nature who loves to share, naturally very shy, but loves public speaking, and if she can inspire just one person to become a warrior not a worrier, she can die a happy woman!

Introduction

This is a book that was written during a time of great change, a period which felt monumentally different, not only for me but also our world, like no other within my life time. It was a time of great spiritual awakening, of adjustment, of transformation. For many globally, it went from the dark night of the soul, to the dark nights of the soul. Energetically things were shifting and have.

It has been a unique time, globally and personally. You may have felt it too. Life came right along, and for some of us, we were knocked off our feet, mentally and emotionally. For others, the dark night of the soul asked us to dig deep. To embark on the uncomfortable but necessary navigation in what has been hibernating or become stagnant within our own lives. Where maybe we have unknowingly chosen to stay in the season of winter, and refuse to entertain the thought of spring.

Life is always calling us to usher in our best selves. To grow and expand with change, (and to continue to reiterate that, that is the one constant in this life). To overcome and become. To be a part of this initiation fully. This life, in the simplicities, the complexities, the unexplainable, the unreasonable, the sensitivities, the heartbreaking, the elation and the mysteries.

This book is about life as an initiation. It is about seeing what we do not want to see, becoming who we think we cannot, it is about crumbling and falling away, only to rebuild what is sacred. This book is about transformation.

Many dark nights of the soul guided me in writing this book. While it didn't seem to take long to write, and in one way appeared to write itself, it asked me to go deeper than my other books, it not only asked, but demanded more of me than ever before.

The words within this book, I share in the hope it stirs something within you. It is my intention, to invite you into the necessary parts of yourself, to connect and reconnect, to experience the dark and the light moments, and be able to integrate them all, as life comes along. It is my hope that these words give you comfort, raise you up in your time of need, keep you connected to what is important and begin to, or continue to allow your soul to guide you through life in what feels like one gigantic initiation.

This book is an invitation for you to overcome, so you can become who you can honestly be in this human experience, to be able to crumble willingly, and fall, to feel and heal, to still rise when you feel weary from battle, and yet sink into your sage wisdom each time ………….

Life comes along.

When Life Comes Along

When exactly does life come along?
In the birth of a child?
Or the magical moment of conception,
or maybe, at the realisation that a life is living within you?

When does life come along?
In the colours that light up a boundless sky at dawn,
or at the goodbye to daylight as the sun bids you, "see you
tomorrow,"
or, in what happens uniquely to every one of us in-between?

When does life come along?
At the time of death of a parent, a child, friend, a loved
one?
In the selfless care in the lead up to their departing,
or at the time of a diagnosis, shocked or expected,
at a knock at your door with tragic news,
or a trembling, reluctant voice with news you are not
prepared for, on the other end of the phone?

When does life come along?
In the "I do"? or in the "you too?" or in the "I understand,"
maybe it is in the "get out!" or "I'm pregnant!"
Or "we lost it." Or maybe even, "I'm so sorry."

When does life come along?
In a loving dog kiss up the side of your face?
Stitch filled laughter of your cat gone wild?
In your first ride on a horse?
Or out bush without direction?

When does life come along?
Your first job? In your first $100.00 in the bank?
First $1000.00? Half a million?
Or in the news you have lost it all?

When does life come along?
When you fall in love? Call it quits?
Leave the nest?
The opening of a door, or the slamming shut of one?

Life comes along in it all,
in the minuscule, and monumental,
in the influential, and ignored.
It fills up every chamber and corner of our heart, then rips
it in two,
only slowly to heal.
Again, and again.

Life comes along in the cooking of a cake,
burnt dinners and laughs,
it comes along in PJ days and A+ essays,
in pieces of music that move you to tears, with hair raising
goosebumps.

Life comes along in the craziest of drives and first kisses,
the touch down and setting foot in a different country.
And, the returning home.
It comes in long lunches with friends, turning into late
dinners,
your first drink, and the twelve step program.

Life comes along in the blowing out of candles,
and getting sunburnt on the beach, wagging school,
sitting at the back of the bus,
and along the track, willingly studying to self-educate.

Life comes along when your body is broken, when you feel it is failing you, and where it feels strong beyond your belief, and you can happily push it to its limits.
It comes along in the rest, on a lazy Sunday,
And when there is a work marathon for which to prepare.

It comes along in the disintegrating of one's own body,
and in the healing which defies all medical reasoning.
It comes along in the obvious moments,
and in the elusive ones, in the macro and micro moments,
whether we decide to float on the surface, or dive deep,
stay in the physical, in plain sight, or slide into the invisible but evident energetic world,
it comes in the beautiful and the insane, the high-level discussions and in the agreements.

The thing is, there is not one thing you cannot think of or experience where it
does not exist. Life is within it all.
In the exceptional, in the bland.
In the black and white and shades of grey.
The ups and downs, insides, and outs.
In the hiding and on the precipice.
Wanted or not,
Life will come along. And does.
It comes along in it all. And keeps on coming.........
Until............ one day...
.... it doesn't.

What Will You Do With Your Time?

The tide rises within,
tears build, and fall,
as the planetary waters respond to the moon,
the wind swirls within, the hurricane of emotions, feelings.
One moment it is a northerly, then a southerly,
an easterly, and eventually a westerly.
The tides, the winds, erode the coastline, gradually chipping
away, sculpting and buffing.
As nature courses through me.
Mine and planetary, I realise my true nature is that of the
great Mother Earth.
Her winds are our change in direction,
her waters are our tears of sorrow and joy,
her mountains are our rock-solid truth.
Her skies are our possibilities,
her soil, our roots to our old knowledge, timeless knowledge.
Her trees are our lungs, her flowers our heart openings,
her seeds, our pure potential.
The stars are remembered places and life times,
The sun, our excitement, our "woohoos!"
The moon, the quiet timeless wisdom.
The babies, new life
The dying, giving back, and moving on.
When we are still, we feel her, we feel it all.
We feel the earth's pulse, her heartbeat, her breath.
We feel the expanse of the galaxies, the cosmos and
vibration of the universe.
We are star seed children,

we are universal beings.
We are the reflection of the divine.
We are God's creation.
We are all knowing.
We are all seeing.
We are all sensing.
We are soul living.
We have within us, the seed, the germination, the stars, the
sun, moon, the rains, the lands,
all the nations in all the galaxies.
Feel into the miracle which is you, which is me.
We are a microscopic speck on a grain of sand,
and yet...... what we do here matters.
So, feel the expanse of the cosmos, the infinite totality
within,
and the unknown but familiar galactic possibilities of all, in
front and around you.
For you are a star seed,
You were created in the image of the holy, the sacred.
You are a miracle of miracles,
and you are here, **now.**
What will you do with your time,
who would you like to become,
when life comes along?

We Do Not Always Get to Choose When Life Changes Happen

When life is going well, we feel we are 'in control,' we tend to embrace change, knowing it is good for us. We are more than likely happy to go with the flow of change. Proudly flying our verbal flag, spouting off, "I love change, it's just what we need." "The only permanent thing in life is change." "When one door closes, another door opens." "She'll be right!"

We receive change well, when we feel we are in control of life. When it is going *our* way.

Then whammo! *Unexpected* change comes along. Change which *we did not choose*. Change we did *NOT* expect. A reorganisation of our outer world, turning our inner world sometimes upside down.

This can be the loss of a loved one, loss of work, home, in divorce or separation, in betrayal, loss of a friendship, a confrontation, anything.

This jolt in change can feel as though the wind has been taken out of your sails, as if you cannot breathe, as if the rug has been pulled out from underneath your feet, as though your heart has stopped or been ripped out altogether.

This, is when life comes along.............. so what do *you* do?

Because it matters.

The outside world will inevitably rock you to your foundations in an instant.
But the collapse and aftershocks should not last a lifetime.

You *are* dying. *I am* dying.

We are *all* dying.

Every day you inch closer to the end of this life.

From the very moment we are born,
we begin to die.

With no crystal ball, and no end point date in
which we know.

Time is valuable. Time is precious.

Finding space within that time is crucial.

Will you spend it complaining, whining,
grumbling, and moaning?

Isn't it worth your while exploring, expanding,
and following your soul's calling?

Because you are dying, I am dying,
we are all dying,

From the moment we are born.

Contemplating, Normalising and Honouring Death

We do not really focus on, or talk about the experiences of death much in our western world. It is not something we ponder, unless it is right in front of us, and for some reason rarely is it discussed deeply, beyond the initial experience we may have witnessed. Being witness to a loved one slipping away from this life is difficult, touching, an honour, confronting, and a great privilege.

The contemplation of death has become a daily inquiry for me. While I have contemplated the process of what I think or feel it might be, for years, especially after having the encounter with our unborn daughter over twenty-five years ago; since the passing of my gorgeous Dad, in March 2023, the enormity of this transformation, the transitioning from birth, existence, to death, fascinates me. This now curiously takes up time in my days.

The moment the soul leaves the body, it is evident, and while the soul is eternal, our earthly body is not. As I have chosen to come here, at this time, on this planet, in this body of mine, just as you have, I would love to love it as much as I can. Cherish it as much as I can. I would love to expand, and open and let as much life in as I possibly can. Don't you?

The more I ponder, the more I go from dabbling in the shallows to wanting to sink into the abyss, of really sitting with the knowing that this physical life **is** temporary. That death, **is** nothing to be feared, it is, I feel, at the time of leaving our physical vehicle, a returning home. Going back to where we came from…….source, divine intelligence, the creator of all things.

The more I sit in the knowing that we are so temporary here on planet Earth in our human body existence, the more I want to, and seem to, honour my human body, and am fascinated by it. The more I contemplate death, the more I appreciate and revere life.

After years of self-punishment and illness, I did learn to fall in love with my physical vehicle and take extra good care of it, with wholesome food, nourishing practices, and a keen awareness of what feels good going in and what does not. But now, contemplating death, my practices have kicked up a notch, and some I have let go altogether.

Fully cherishing and appreciating my now alive body and opportune circumstances in every single moment of every single day.

Western society seems to have a strong aversion to death and dying. We fear it, do not talk about it in depth, often keeping it locked away, or at arm's length. While other countries, traditions and spiritual practices openly mourn, accept, and I have no doubt, still may feel confronted with death, they are willing to fully experience these moments, as a natural part of life.

When my Dad passed at home in his own bed just after midnight, on a Wednesday night, with my Mum holding his hand, I was the first to arrive just in time to witness his body's last out breath, which in and of itself was such an honour to share with him and Mum. They were there to see my first breath in this life and I was there to see his last.

The family came straight down. My brother, my husband, and our two boys. We were all there within the hour.

After the formalities of police and doctor's sign off, we were given a phone number to phone so my father could be picked up.

It was an emphatic "*no*" from my mother.

He was not to be picked up right away. Mum wanted him there with her and us. Besides, we could '*feel*' him still there. He had gone, but not yet left.

While the soul had left his body, it had not left the room, or their home. Although all that was left was his peaceful physical form, face smooth, young looking, free of pain, worry, and tension, the soul which animated my Dad, was no longer in his earthly vessel; we could still *feel* him.

As Dad lay peacefully, all the pain gone from his face and body, we sat around and cried of course, we laughed, we held his hands, we cuddled up to him. As we had not been able to touch him for well over a year due to the intolerable pain he had endured – he could touch us occasionally but we could not touch him.

We come from a touchy family, so this time was excruciating, certainly for him, and for us too, to not be able to touch the one you love.

Early that morning, Dad's sister, my aunt, joined us, along with my father in-law and two of the most magnificent carers we had experienced or known. They shared with us a time not unique, as we all die, and have had someone close to us pass on, but unique in the sense and way in which we shared this sacred time with Dad. Together.

We kept him at home for nearly twelve hours. We had time with him together, and each of us having alone time. We laughed at jokes which we felt and saw him laughing along with us. We cried tears of loss and at the same time relief for him having left behind the intensely agonising pain of his human body. Sadly, with no help from the palliative care for pain relief, like so many others we have come to know, we had to journey much of this road alone, together.

We whispered into his ears our deepest of appreciation and awe at his selfless fatherhood, his wisdom, and for the years of his experience shared with us in this life time.

My father in-law and I sat with Dad, I had breakfast sitting on his bed, we chatted, shared, laughed, cried, and felt relief, often all at the same time. It was an incredibly touching time to have shared with my father in-law and will always be deeply cherished.

My brother brought his eldest daughter, my niece down. She at the tender age of seven years. While tentative at first, and with no force by us, she entered the room. While yes, there were tears, natural of course, she handled herself as only a well-adjusted, seven-year-old does.

She was intrigued, she asked questions, she touched his hands, she laughed, she cried, she drew him a picture and collected magpie feathers from the front lawn for him, (just as they had both done together throughout her childhood), to be with him as he went on the next part of his journey.

When we do not put our fears, scars and misconstrued ideas and stories onto our children, they handle circumstances in which we so often deem too traumatic or not for children, with a childlike curiosity, balance, a wisdom, and simplicity which seem beyond their years. Naturally.

My niece offered by her own volition to help the funeral director by carrying the paperwork in folders as she followed them carrying Dad out to the funeral car, as he left his home for the last time.

Twelve precious hours we had with Dad after he took his last breath. To us, this felt completely normal, to others we have shared this with, there have been raised eyebrows and an uncomfortable "oh, did you really?" and others, "good on you." "Wow, that's amazing, I didn't know you could do that!"

A very dear friend of mine, whom I met just under two years after she lost her husband, shared with me her touching experience with her husband after I had shared about having this time with my Dad.

She too, along with her husband's blessing did things their way. When her husband passed away at their home, she kept him home for three days, crying with him, sitting with him, laying with him, praying with him, and talking with him.

A week before his funeral, she made adornments from things from the garden and she welcomed the chance to put them on his body. She also chose for him to be dressed in a lovely piece of linen gauze instead of clothes, and the funeral home was more than happy to honour her request.

She shared that when it came time to adorn his body with the natural jewellery, which she had made, if felt like such a natural thing to be doing, and something she felt, should become common in our society.

In her own words, "My husband joked, "make sure you leave the air conditioner on!" We had talked about it.

It was the way it just had to be, it felt so normal. We are missing out on so much more if we are just handing over our loved one to a funeral home.

To witness a last breath of someone is a phenomenal experience, and to help prepare them is not only an honour, but I feel it helps our own healing process.

I hope people find the strength and find the beauty, in being with someone at the end of their life, and not rush the process, but honour the space in what is a remarkably sacred experience."

I could not agree more. To witness, and lovingly be involved with a loved one's passing onto the next part of their journey is such an honour. To affectionately and thoughtfully spend time with them, so as not to rush the process, and prepare for our human goodbyes is something which must be experienced. I personally will never forget that time, as I know my dear friend will not either.

It is my wish, that this natural process becomes more normalised as time goes on, where we do not shy away from this one-way ticketed life, but give thanks to the treasured and miraculous relationship your loved one has graced you with, during this ever so human life.

Death is inevitable. It is certain.

We must, I feel, normalise death, and we do not within our modern society. What is inevitable and unavoidable, rather than rushing our loved one off, why not honour them by spending a little time with them even in death, even if in traumatic and unforeseen circumstances. When my mother was with a friend who passed from a horrific accident, there was a lace like fabric covering his injuries, yet still his face looked beautiful, which helped his mother, father, and siblings.

We have no visual sand in the hour glass for us to observe for our timely or untimely departure, or that of our loved ones. Sometimes there can be preparation, and other times, like the drop of a hat, it happens without warning.

Knowing it is coming, consciously knowing, can change the way we look at how we approach, and appreciate life.

I feel when we really start contemplating death, particularly *our own* death, feeling into *our own* mortality *without* the melancholy attitude, *without* the morbid drama.............. *then* we start living.

We are alive now. Now. We are alive in our human existence. Knowing that everything ends, everything has a season including us in our human body. Some seasons are shorter than others and some are shorter *for* others.

One of my yoga teachers started every workshop with "you are all terminal, you are all dying, including me, so why not let us start really living? Let us really be **in** the earthly body, starting now."

When we start living, really living, all our senses come alive! Not only the five senses, but well beyond!

If we dedicate ourselves to being fully alive, here, and now, and *live* fully alive, with not only our seeing eyes, but with our inner eye wide open, not closed, we would then walk with intuitive intention and an organic spring in our step. With an aliveness, not like we are the walking dead. We would then experience all the craziness, mess, responsibility, elation, magnificence, impermanence, beautifully transient, important, unimportant, trepidation, frozen fears, habits, what matters and what does not, in this ordinary yet extraordinary thing called life.

The Clock is Ticking

We are dying. You are dying, I am dying, we are all dying. We are terminal.
The clock is ticking.
What are you doing with your time?
What are you going to do with your remaining time?
What do you keep talking about doing, and never do?
What do you keep doing and want to stop?

Knowing you, me, everyone around us is dying, invites us to reflect on 'true meaning.'
This life is finite, **no-one** gets out alive!

What matters to you? What does not?
For God's sake, could you be in this present moment? Now? Here? Within these pages? These snippets, these musings, these ponderings?
These maybes and must not's, yes's and no's, not only make up my life, they make up yours.
Do they matter? YES. And some others? Definitely NO.
What do you want?
What do you really want? What do you want to do?
What do you want to try?
What do you want to achieve?
What do you want to let go of?
Where do you want to go?
Who do you want to spend time with?
Do you want to laugh more?
Do you want to cry?
Do you want to move more? Your body, or geographically?

Would you want to spend time with you?
Would you want to marry you?
Would you want to be your friend?
Would you want to rely on you?
Would you want to love you?

Being witness to my darling Dad's painful journey, (what seemed to him, I am sure, like God forsaken suffering in those final years leading up to his release, for the next part of his journey), after arriving in time to witness the air leaving his lungs for the last time in his human body, things changed for me.

Life changed.
What matters to me right now is that I write and share this book.
What does not matter to me? Is that you do not read it.
But…… I hope you do, for you.
Because it all matters, and at the same time nothing matters all.
What matters to you?
Let us dive into the depths of life, and take the time to also play in the shallows ……..
And let's find out!

Love yourself enough to go beyond your
limited thinking of yesterday,

Love yourself enough to excel beyond
what is expected of you,

Love yourself enough to go beyond your
parents' limitations.

Love yourself enough to have one week
away *on your own,*

at least once in your life,

love yourself enough to be content in
your own company.

Always Running Late?

Love yourself enough.......

It is not only disrespectful to others who constantly wait for you, more importantly, it is disrespectful to yourself.

Love yourself enough to show up to yourself ……. On time!

Love yourself enough to lighten your load.

You were never meant to carry this weight alone.

Love yourself enough to choose wisely, inner wisdom nudges you constantly and always, with love.

Love yourself enough to know every decision you make, you live. *Every decision, you live.*

Love yourself enough to realise you may not create every experience you encounter, but you do create the way in which you experience it, no matter how trivial, whether it be mental, physical, emotional, or spiritual.

Love yourself enough to stop. To deliberately create a pause in your day.

Love yourself enough to know it is within the pause, new ideas are birthed, inspiration is born.

Love yourself enough to begin, *something, anything, just begin*. When you open to something new, the old falls away, it dies.

Love yourself enough to let go, to not fear destruction, the death of something, anything, an idea, a construct, or habit, allows *room* for the birth of something new.

Love yourself enough to sit, to be quiet. Do not fear stillness, stillness is where the richness lives.

Love yourself enough to be vulnerable.

Love yourself enough, to bare your soul to a loved one. Sharing, openness, trust, communication deepens your experience in this life. Life is meant to shared .... Deeply.

Love yourself enough to simplify, complexity is the enemy of peace. You want peace? Simplicity is everything.

Busy-ness does not matter, chasing your tail does not matter.

Does achievement matter? Does productivity matter?

That is up to you.......

All I have come to know, though, for sure .... without a doubt ....

Is that peace matters.

The Tamed and Untamed Mind
Friend or Foe?

Where will you go today my friend?

Where will you go today my friend?
A pondering? A day dream?
Simply rest under a rain drenched, sun-soaked tree?
As the droplets shimmer and take their time,
to fall from the leaves.

Where will you go today my friend?
A blanket on your knee, cuppa in hand?
With the loving look of man's best friend, locking eyes with
yours?
As you simply wonder what your furry friend might be
thinking.

Where will you go today my friend?
A rhyme? A riddle? A note, a chain of melody?
Time for play?
With no outcome needed today.
Just play.

Where will you go today my friend?
A "she'll be right?" A "let's do this!"
A quiet sit and do nothing? Simply just sit,
With the content-'est' of smiles soft on your face.

Where will you go today my friend?
Be in the best company of quiet meanderings,

of soft reflections? With lavish space and soft
furnishings for the one invaluable tenant? You.

You are free to roam today my friend,
You have earned the respect; I hold you in high regard.
Stroll, ramble, and potter, whatever comes across your
mind.
As I know you will be more than willing to venture back,
when I ask.
We have both earned the freedom, in this moment,
And again, tomorrow. Another new now moment.

What Are You Doing Today My Foe?

What are you doing today my foe?
Let us jump straight into a mire of decades worth of fault?
And stir the coffee pot with a bitter taste of blame.
You will drive the same way to work reluctantly, dragging
what is left of inspiration behind you.

What are you doing today my foe?
I thought I would fill you with constipation of thought,
repetitive thought, constant thought, reams of thought,
tiresome thought, melancholy thought,
and wash it down with a cup of the "why me?"

What are you doing today my foe?
Well, I thought the same as yesterday,
and because you did the same as the day before, the week
before,
year before. I thought we would simply repeat.
I assumed that is what you would want?

What are you doing today my foe?
Judge another willingly, then willingly judge another,
and while we are at it, we may as well,
judge you.

What are you doing today my foe?
Sleep late, drag yourself around,
misery loves company, so you believe,
curtains drawn, sit on the phone, scroll, and scroll again,
and together watch others live their life,
as you *think* yours away.

What are you doing today my foe?
Restrict your thoughts to the same familiar ones,
spice it up with a little regret, add a pinch of envy,
on the whole today, lets stay in the familiar,
let's stay in the safe harbour............. And do it all again
tomorrow.

"Sometimes I sit and think, and sometimes I just sit."

This is a quote from a cherished client, who has become a dear friend, she shared this with me during one of those heart to heart, profound conversations we so often share. She remembers her Grand-father sitting her on his knee and sharing this with her, it was she who shared it with me, and it is me who is sharing it with you.

This quote, on the surface seems so simple. However, when you let it sit with you, and you with it, its depth starts to reveal itself. The practice of these words, has the ability, to carve out a life practice in meditative naturalness, in openness, in simplicity……. in peace.

**Tomorrow is not promised,
So, what matters to you today?**

One Day Will Be Your Last

One day, life will *NOT* come along.
Eventually, for you, there will be one last sunrise,
one last sunset.
A good night kiss from your love, will, eventually be your last.
One day, there will be, one last hug,
one last cuppa,
one last laugh,
one last loving pat of your dog,
one last slap of the snooze button.
One last holiday to plan,
one last "I love you" that passes your lips.
One day, that little flirtatious look you give your love, will not be.
One day, something will be your last.
Which one? And when? No one can tell you. No one.
One day the turn of a last page mid-read of a novel, will be your last.
One sigh, one last movie, one last night, one last day.
One day, one breath will be your last.
One day, will be your very last one.
One day, life will *NOT* come along.

A Small Life?

Sometimes I feel I have lived a small life, a lovely life but a small life, a fulfilled life (most of the time) but a small life. And as I wander the world, and ponder my inner world, I wonder……….. do I live this small life because I am fearful of living a big life? A huge life? A colossal life? And, what does that even mean?

To be honest, the answer eludes me, to be deeply honest, am I really scared to find out the answer?

Did I choose a small life?

Did a small life choose me?

Did fear dictate the smallness of my life?

The answer is yet to be found, felt, or experienced.

Could my life have been edgier? Could it have been more worldly? Could it be experienced more deeply………

Have I met enough interesting people? Have I bought enough, sold enough, moved enough, travelled enough? Did I revel in the brand names and the stories and people behind them. Did I celebrate in the homemade delights in food, clothes, handbags, art?

Did I feel the soul who made them? Did I pay homage to them, their ideas? Their talent? To their creativity?

Have I enjoyed the finer things in life, fine wine, gorgeous jewellery? Knowing also, someone created these outstanding pieces.

Did I delight enough in my face being sculptured, lifted, and pulled back to being years younger, as the g-forces of a spectacularly fast car put me back in the seat?

Did I savour the moment of knotted and matted hair riding a motorbike helmet free?

Have I missed an opportunity in saying no to going out to dinner with others, preferring in that moment to have a shared shower with my husband, make love, and curl up on the couch with a wine, watch a movie with my man?

Have I missed opportunities and savoured memories with my family by saying yes to others?

Was I pegged as an imposter when I looked confident, yet really, physically with my knees buckling with nerves?

Have I said yes enough? Or too many times?

Did I say no too many times? Or not enough?

When I was asked to break out, did I recoil and stay in?

When I was forced to stay in, did I rebel and breakout? Enough?

When I was asked to speak, did I speak well? Did I speak up? Did I respect? Did I listen?

When I was invited to teach, did I predict, pre-empt, observe, pay enough attention? Did my students feel safe?

Did I let our boys know just how proud of them I am? Enough? Did they feel loved enough? Seen and heard? Enough? Did I ask enough or too much? Did I listen to their dreams?

Have I laid on the ground enough? Did I daydream enough? Too much, or too little?

Have I talked myself out of things before I have started?

Was there ever a balance to be struck? Or was I struck off, knowing I would never find the balance? Did I strike myself off?

Were there moments where I felt I missed the boat? Many moments? Absolutely.

Have all of these made me feel as though my life is small?

When I sit with this, not think about it, but sit with it…………….. when I sit with all these questions, there is a sense I could have done better, could have done more, been more, done less, gone out more, stayed home more, said more, said less, listened more, bought less, it goes on, and yet ……

I feel content. Wonderfully content.

Is that just for now? Or will I feel content in the future?

And in the meantime, is my life small, or just cozy?

Who knows, but I am amazingly comfortable in waiting to find out.

Are You "Damming Up" Your Life?

Have you ever watched water? Really watched water? Have you ever really studied water? Observed it?

What did you notice?

When you watch a river, a lake, a pond, the ocean, a creek, a waterfall............. What do you observe?

Could you see yourself in this body of water? I think water is wise, and when we really sit and watch it, when we really *see* it, its patterns, its character, its path, its health, it can carry messages for us.

A river finds its direction, and goes with it. A river is always in flow. It can be unpredictable, it can, when the weather changes, and storms arise, become violent. White rapids, can twist and turn, no matter what obstacles try and stop it, no matter what resistance it encounters, it will and does find a way around.

It can be gentle, ever so subtle, with the gentlest of flow, and yet the rapids can come out of nowhere. No matter, a river carves out its own way.

A lake when calm, is often referred to a mill pond. Meaning it looks like a mirror. The quality of a mirror is that it reflects things. It reflects its surroundings.

A pond can be small by comparison of other bodies of water, yet never when we look at a pond, do we feel cheated by its size. Its perceived 'smallness.' A pond teams with life, shallow enough to let the sunlight reach the bottom, so an ever-changing community of animals and often plants, can grow right across and thrive. A small universe of creatures and micro-organisms can live and flourish for many years in a small but lively pond.

The ocean, a magnificent continuous body of water, which surrounds the lands of this magnificent planet, a salty life filled blue, with mysteries and depths, some still to be discovered. Its contrast and beauty, the complexity, and ornamental details it carves out on its shores are nothing short of stunning, magnificent, and simply breathtaking.

The gentle rock of the ocean can lull you to sleep, the deep swell can be, and sometimes is, energising to watch but can feel tentative to be on, the crashing of waves can be spectacular to witness and terrifying at the same time. There is something about this salty body of water which has been the inspiration and heartache for many. The terror, spiritual inquiry, myths, stories, poems, music, movies, and personal growth still expand our minds, ignite our imagination, inspires our creativity and heals our heart.

It is tumultuous, calm, stormy, beautiful, shallow, a deep watery world, some of which we still have not yet discovered. With its many hues of colour, it has healing, therapeutic, and meditative qualities. I often wonder, with qualities like these, do we feel such fascination with the ocean because it is much like ourselves? Our emotions, our personality, our subconscious? Or is it because, we are mainly made up of water? On the surface all is perceived busy, the activity of the mind, our thoughts, our emotions, our stresses, our sensations, and the depth, where all is quiet, our true nature, where we have befriended our mind, and for the most part, mastered it. There is no chaos, just stillness, only calm.

A creek acting as a drain, helps to reduce the impact of flooding. No matter how narrow, or trickle, a creek is, it can still be home to many birds and types of fish. The creeks, like their big brother the river, represent transformation and the flow of time.

Even creeks can have rocks and pebbles in which the water must navigate to keep moving through. It also helps to purify water, filtering as it winds along, enabling the water to remain clean and energised.

Waterfalls...... What have you noticed about waterfalls........ no matter how small, whether it is a small drop just from a few rocks into a creek, or a huge, spectacular, jaw dropping phenomena?

Water falls do not resist!!! There is no resistance, just flow. You cannot help but feel a sense of purification and renewal when you stand in front of, or even better, under a waterfall. The waterfall is the full representation of letting go, of cleansing. But what I notice most about waterfalls is they do not resist. So why do we?

Remember we all have choice.

You have choice, and if you think you do not have a choice, then that is your choice to think you do not have a choice.

Allow water to be a reminder for you daily. Whether you can get near an ocean, walk near a lake, skip across a creek, or be lucky enough to live near a waterfall. If you do not have any of these accessible to you physically, then listen to water through music, or podcasts, or have it as a screen saver on your computer.

So, when life comes along, because it does, and it *will*, look to the messages in water. Could you find your stillness like the depths of the ocean, or maybe turn rage of a large ocean, into passion, and courage needed to forge ahead or stand up for what is right.

Could you go with the flow, no matter how small or slow the trickle may seem or feel, just like the stream? Can you purify and let go of what is not serving you? Start small like the creek. Maybe just let go for the day! Purify your meals, your mind. Then start with your week, bit by bit you will gain the knowledge to put into practice what you need to know **and do,** when life comes along.

Stop "damming up" your life and let it flow. Listen to the call of your flow, of your river, find your stillness like the depths of the ocean. And remember the waterfall does not resist, so why do you?

I loved this quote so much, which was shared with me by a lovely friend after she stumbled across it herself. I had to share it with you.

She is someone who, through her words, through conversation, invites me to delve a little deeper into reflection. While I do not spend a lot of time with her, the time I do, she always leaves me a little gift to contemplate.

"Waterfalls wouldn't sound so melodious if there were no rocks in their way."

Rishabh Gautam

Your life is
your initiation!

Could It Become a Dance?

You were created to experience this life fully.

When you wrestle with it, you tire yourself to living fully.

Your dreams become nightmares, or the visions stop completely, leaving you feeling dead inside.

Could the wrestle become a dance instead? Maybe even eventually a finely tuned dance? Like the visual poetry and wisdom in the flow, but concise martial arts.

Could the wrestle become the waltz?

Could the waltz be the wise teacher of confidence, of learning the skill of timing. The waltz is the only dance that uses ¾ timing. Could you learn the power of knowing? Knowing when to lead and when to follow?

Could the wrestle become the tango? Could you learn to become completely in the moment?

All too often we think and do not feel, therefore sending us deeper into the wrestling ring.

Could the tango teach you to feel, not think?

Could the tango if you allowed it, teach you to fine tune your balance, *your* balance, in life?

Could the wrestle become the jive?

With the pace of the jive, just like life, could it teach you and encourage you, and reinforce to you that it is practice, practice, practice?

Willingness, consistency, and persistence is the key.

The jive is fast, quick in tempo. The gift? Teaching you to be light on your feet, light in life.

The salsa? Salsa is the Spanish word for sauce. The secret sauce to life maybe?

Love, compassion, variety, and child-like curiosity.

Could the salsa just simply teach you that if you make a mistake, that is okay, and you *could* just start again? That anything on the dance floor is a challenge, like life, and the steps that were once so foreign, begin to become familiar.

What once daunted you, now becomes easy, and you begin to literally **master** them. Confidence grows, then you find a new dance comes along with new steps to learn, and you begin again.

So rather than wrestle with life, could you learn to dance with life instead of wrestling against it?

Learn the steps, glide across the dance floor of life, stand tall, in your mind and heart, be proud. Connect with another, get lost in the moment, stay grounded, but move your feet, and allow the lessons in the rhythm of dance, *any dance*, move you.

Allow the rhythm of life move you and through you at the same time, until you become the dance, until you become alive with **LIFE**.

Dance with life and *allow* yourself to be danced by life. Mess up? Lose your steps? Miss your cue? Don't worry. Do not overthink, simply begin again.

In Conversation with Spirit

I don't think I can……
Oh, but you can,
But how?
Just listen to me,
Do you really exist?
I exist in everything you do.
But I cannot feel you.
Slow your walk, I am here walking with you.
But I cannot see you.
Open your inner eye, you will see me.
I cannot hear you though.
I am in the space in between your thoughts, the gaps of silence.
There is no space! I cannot do this anymore, nothing changes!
My dear one, you are getting in your own way, you are keeping these spaces filled
with unimportant things, everything which is meaningless.
Lean into me, let me hold you.
But it is important!
Is it? Will you remember what keeps you awake now in ten years' time?
Isn't it heavy? Too loud? Too cluttered? Too busy? Too tight? Compressed?
Yes! Yes! Yes!
Feel into this resistance. This is you pushing against me,
When you resist me, it feels uneasy.
Feel those niggles?
Yes.
Feel the nudges?
Yes, I cannot sleep.

That is me. Let me rock you to sleep.
Allow me to guide you into your dreams
I am IN your dreams.
I am in the nourishing foods you grow, make, and create,
I am in the colours and fabrics you wear,
I am in the notes and melodies of the music your ears dance upon,
I am in the vegetable garden you sow and reap,
I am in the sand in between your toes,
I am in the first sip of tea,
I am in the colours on a canvas,
I am in the language you speak,
I am in the words on this page,
I am in the thundery clouds,
I am in the wisdom of all animals,
I am in the seasons,
I am in mysterious depths of the oceans,
I am in the shine of the sun,
I am in the face of the moon,
I am in the bee collecting the pollen,
I am in the soil, the seed, the forests.
I am in every inhale, every exhale, and the pause in between,
I am in your lungs, your bones, your heart, your flesh, your creation.
I am everywhere. Everywhere and in everything,
Including you.
Allow me to guide you.

When you no longer turn your back on me, when you decide........
to finally choose to sit with me, space will be created, and what has been closed within you will open. All will open within you and for you.

But how?
Not how............ but why.

Why do you want to come back to centre?
Why do you want to connect and re-connect?
Why do you want feel at peace?
Why do you want to feel strong?
Why do you want to feel spacious?
Why do you want to feel at one with all?
Trust me my child, you find the why, and the how will appear.
How is in the head, why is in the heart, the soul.
It is your head that has separated you from me, from all that is.
I am always in your why.
Your "why" will, if you allow, lead you back to your whole self,
where nothing is separate within you or from you.
Let go of the resistance, what you resist, will persist.
The pain is in the resistance.
Let go.
So, breathe now, and ....
Let go my dear one.
Let go.

"You learn the most
about yourself,
when you are alone"

Life 'Bytes' from Two Types of Wisdom

Intuitive Wisdom and Deep Wisdom

At the time of writing this, it had been just over a year since my Dad passed on from this earthly plane. It was heart wrenching to watch the demise of the human body in someone you adore and who has helped shape you. Who was there for every wobble, every fall, who, even though sometimes found it tough to understand what was or had transpired in my brother's or my life, you just knew it was still a safe place. It was kept in the vault of silence. Never to be shared, unless we chose to.

He had the ability to get down on another's level, and still raise them up. Lift them to beyond what they thought they could do or be. He had the uncanny knack of reading people, knowing what they needed, even before they knew it themselves. Mastering the art of the ultimate 'pep talk,' and inspirational talk, eye to eye, heart to heart, from a father to a child, father to a teenager, and on to father to an adult child.

He was elegant in his word choices, articulate, and even when a teenager, knowing full well he was the last person I wanted to take advice from, he intentionally sowed the seeds, for my brother and I to flourish. Even as a rebellious teenager, I knew he approached topics, and handled things differently from other Dads. While he was conservative in so many areas; typically around the topic of sex, my Mum handled those very open, no holds barred, conversations, he had a wisdom about him, a light, a grounded 'ness,' solidarity, the deepest of love and sacrifice regarding his family.

He educated himself, bettered himself, and found mentors in his early years. He reached for the stars and encouraged us to do the same. Dad surrounded himself with people he perceived or were smarter than he was. Not only did he surround himself with people emotionally and academically smarter than himself, he studied them. Therefore, nurturing and nourishing his own well of knowledge, so he could put everything he was learning into practice. Remembering knowledge is useless unless we put it into action. He mastered this.

Too many things to share here, literally, and many private and very sacred, but a few I would like to share with you in the hope they stir something in you as they did me, not only in my early years but deepened in my young adult life, and are now more important than ever in my 'mid' life.

Here is something for *you* to ponder. I still not only ponder them, but completely immerse myself in these conversations at times. Allowing them to permeate not only my thoughts, but my actions and life, with his wise words and his teaching by example often *without* words, he shared with me and I am sure also my brother.

While I remember full well my Mum saying to Dad, seeing our irritation at times, "You cannot put an old head on young shoulders!" "Let them find their own way!" While yes, we were irritated at times, and we did choose to have selective hearing when the pep talks were often the last things we wanted to hear, yet somehow, they entered our psyche. They may have even saved my life. But there is no doubt, they have and continue to make an impact not only on my life, but that of our boys, because they were given the blueprints of these life 'bytes,' so they can forge ahead in life tuning into their own intuitive and deep wisdom.

These are some of the wisdom 'bytes' he raised us with, they always had a common thread;

"When you change (try to fit in) for others, you are lying to yourself."

It may not seem like much in one moment in time, however, if you continue to change for others in order to fit in, or be accepted, you will eventually feel stifled, exhausted, cheated, fake, and the lie you lay down with when you close your eyes, at the end of the day, will eventually eat you from the inside out.

"You cannot live a brave and courageous life without disappointing others."

"If you want to forge ahead on an undiscovered road, you must be prepared to disappoint others."

In other words, if you want to find and follow your True North, no matter how outrageous an idea it may seem, you will inevitably disappoint others. If you do not, you are living a life of people pleasing, and trust me, that is no way to live a fulfilling life. In fact, it will suck the life right out of you.

Personal growth, emotional and spiritual growth, growth in business, or a completely new venture, can feel lonely at times. But, if you know *why* you are forging ahead, *why* you are climbing that metaphorical mountain, or real one! *Why* you do not want mediocrity, then you will have times where you will take the solo trek, but you will not feel lonely.

You will need to venture into unknown territory, do things most others will never do, see things differently, see opportunity where others see only obstacles, chances where others only see failure, take huge action where others only make excuses, and walk through the opening of a door through divine timing.

"You are too smart for that."

This, what I saw as a flippant and irritating comment from a father to a daughter, was to say the least......... irritating. Back then, I only ever saw it as him trying to halt my fun in some way. But these words and the energy which is behind them still serves me well to this day.

While he was not asking me to never take risks or live a dull life, he was asking me to think for myself.

Both my parents and my maternal grandmother taught me *how to think not what to think.* And I am so beyond grateful for these words of wisdom. Sadly, learning how to think is not currently taught in our schools, as it should be.

Right thought as Krishna Murti calls it, is fluid, free, moveable, it sustains us, it has life energy running through it.

Right thought is rigid, it is institutional in its teachings, it is solid, with a 'no question' attitude to it.

This came to light like never before in my life time, in the last few years or so, where en masse, we were taught 'what' to think, a few brave and courageous souls followed their intuitive and instinctive 'how' to think. Now we see others worldwide, opening to their inner knowledge and wisdom and living from a place of right thinking, not right thought. How refreshing.

When life comes along, tune into your own well of intuition, into your own knowingness.

"You are too smart for that." Is not big noting yourself, it is not that you are better than anyone else, it is not something you need to shout from the roof tops, but when you are lovingly honest with yourself, dig deep, reach for the sky, go beyond your perceived limits, get out of your comfort zone, stay your moral compass. Because, you know, at times, **you are too smart for that!**

"When you fall, because you will, when you fail, because you will, or........ "If you ever have children.......the lessons just begin."

When you fall, when you fail, because you most certainly will do both, and most definitely when you have children, the lessons just begin. Dad directly and indirectly taught me this. And so did having children!! There is no step-by-step instruction book about life, there is no 'go to' handbook where you can turn to the chapter you are needing, regarding this, what feels like the elusive steps you need to take next. Such a book does not exist.

Whenever I didn't understand what point my Dad was trying to make in a moment, whenever I chose *not* to understand, or listen to what he was trying to in-still in me, or what mini but powerful wisdom he was imparting to me, he would often start a pep talk with, "One day, when you have children, you will begin to understand, you will come to know what I am talking about". Or "You will fall, I know, and at times you **feel** you are failing, dig deep, breathe, look at how far you have come, look at what you have already accomplished........" or "When you look back on your life, would you rather have failed than not have tried at all? You would rather know, than always wonder."

It was comments like these, that enabled my inner dialogue to remain open. Even in my teenage 'ism' years.

My Dad's wisdom was two-fold, and they both overlapped and interconnected, perfectly woven to create an environment, our home, with the depth of learned and intuitive wisdom.

These are tough lessons. Even now. They are so simple, that their simplicity is often what stumps us. But deep down, deep where no one else sees, deep where we very rarely explore and very rarely honour, you know these life 'bytes' *already* for yourself.

Intuitive wisdom lives in many of us. It resides deep within. It is a knowing, which sometimes we cannot even explain. Children have it naturally, and utilise it until it is schooled out of them. It is something we must encourage our younger generations to use and enhance. For those of us who have come to rely on our intuitive wisdom, know it is fully appreciated and worked, daily, it goes without saying that it is as natural as breathing. It never leads us astray when we truly tune in.

We are close to spirit, the cosmos, God, whatever you wish to call it, when we are in tune with our intuition, honour it *and* use it. It is the universal, spirit wisdom which whispers to us, giving us the prompts and nudges when needed.

Deep wisdom comes from life experience. It comes from lessons learned; it comes from contemplating life experiences not dwelling on them. With deep wisdom, we know we are never done learning, we are forever the student, and through our perceived failures we know we are in no position to judge another.

We know life can be hard. Damn difficult at times. Bloody heart-wrenching. And, let us be honest, it can feel as though it damn well sucks. When we draw on deep wisdom, we do not presume to know all the answers, we have no need to gloat. And with deep wisdom, which continues to enhance in a life with awareness, we know we will continue to make mistakes in life; however, we also know we will recover from them with an even deeper wisdom, than when we entered the lesson.

Whether my Dad knew consciously or subconsciously, it does not matter. What matters is, on some level, he knew he had to pass on what he had come to know, with us and our children. So, we and our children, can pass it down the line for future generations. So, our children's children can learn what deep wisdom can do not only for themselves, but for others.

From my father to me, to you………….. I hope you delve into your wisdom, both, intuitive and deep, build upon them, listen to them. And allow them to guide you…………. when life comes along.

If you dare to only have
one dream for this life,
If you dare to only
set one goal for this
life............
Then dare to *choose* to
live a life of substance.

In one anguished point in time………

In an unforeseeable next move, or the inability
to take a deep breath…………

In a changeable instant which rocks a heart
that yearns for stability and safety………

In the agonising snapshots of life……

It is in the learning from the emotionally taxing,
challenging and tricky moments…….

Learning in the moments which *are*
not going so well,

That is where the power lies.

Equal and Opposite Reactions, Giant Magnets, and Mirrors

The third law of motion, "for every action, there is an equal and opposite reaction."

Sooooooo............. Every action you put out into the world there is an equal and opposite reaction.

There are many examples of Newton's third law of motion, but one I love, is that "when a swimmer pushes off the side of a pool, the wall pushes back on the swimmer with an equal and opposite force."

The energy of what you say, of what you do, of who you are, is travelling out into the world, and that energy is always coming back to you, at the same level and rate at which you send it out. This physical formula is not just a scientific formula, it applies a hundred percent to our lives.

Once again, for every action, there is an equal and opposite reaction. All the way through and within your life.

You are also a giant magnet.

Every time you get fired up, hurt, or angry, those feelings and emotions do not just dissipate into nothingness; they do not just disappear into some invisible vapor. No. If not dealt with in a conscious way, the energy of them come back to you. Not allowing life to move through you, where you sometimes unconsciously hold on to an experience, it is stored in the body. The body **remembers**, and the 'body keeps score,' physically and emotionally, it feels like you simply cannot take on anymore, because 'seeds have been planted' within your own being, within your own body.

Some of us, including me, in past years, have pushed blame, hurts and traumas down so far, they are in the 'proverbial basement,' seemingly out of view. But .... there will come a time, trust me, where your body will have no more room to stock pile the archives of pain and suffering any longer. And that my friend, is where there will be a seemingly benign comment, that will induce a hurricane of an outburst, where you will 'fly off the handle.' Where your body comes to a point where it is full, the energetic, emotional, and of course physical body. It is not a fullness and overflowing of goodness, or wellbeing, it becomes full and burdened by hurt, blame, guilt, and toxic secrets, it cannot hold anymore and you will erupt. It will always surface somewhere. Your body will always let you know the truth and will *always* win. It may not always show up instantaneously, but again......... your body keeps score **always.** For every action, there is an equal and opposite reaction, and at the same time, this energy will pull in, will be passed on, or pushed onto another, and, onto another, whether it be through words, or behaviour, and, *will always come back to you in some way.*

For me, I was tossed into the 'university of life' when my body said "enough! I am full." This is where my body clearly failed me, stopped me, seemingly turned on me. And so, the lessons began. This is where we often see 'break downs,' or autoimmune health challenges, sleepless nights, puffiness, and inflammation. Our body is so wise, a finely tuned instrument with a divinely designed intricate computer system with its own intelligence.

When I am doing a one on one with an individual in body work, breathwork or coaching, that individual may be, and often will, be visibly 'hiding,' hoping I cannot 'see' and even lying to themselves and of course to me! That, they are alright, but ……... their body tells a different story, one hundred percent of the time. The body *never* lies. Their words do not match their energy as mine did not regarding my situation in health. But it was the energy behind my language and private thoughts which kept the law of attraction alive and well, even though I did not like what I was attracting!

Mirrors

Brett and I always told our boys as they were growing up, the world will reflect the energy of their thoughts, feelings, and behaviour. Just like a mirror.

In fact, not like a mirror, *but a mirror*. You will see, get back and experience exactly what you are sending out. You are responsible for the energy you put out into the world, and whether you believe it or not, it is just how it works, and will always do so. It is that simple.

Equal and opposite reactions, giant magnets and mirrors on the surface appear not to be related, or similar. And they are not, but they are............ because no matter which one we are living in, in any given moment, we are the ones who benefit, receive, and experience the reaction, law of attraction, or reflection, in that split second. Or the flow on affect, where we will still experience our past energetic behaviour, in the future.

We live what we create.

The Lost Art of Listening

Seldom do we learn when we speak, and very rarely do we gain insight when we speak, but a lot happens when we learn to listen. Sadly, most people start to speak only as a segue to the subject **they** want to talk about. On rare occasions do they even listen, and once in a blue moon they *may be* capable of listening.

All too often they really are just like a 'tree gecko with mouth wide open,' just waiting to verbally pounce, interrupt and talk over the top of another, trying to get *their* point across. They may look like they are listening, but in fact, they are simply waiting for that minute pause to say what they want to say next.

My husband is a great listener. He will never talk over the top of another. The same respect, however, has not always been reciprocated. I have heard him say over the years, "it's why I don't say a lot, why would I waste my breath, my energy, my words, my voice, when they are not listening anyway, I'll save it for those who are respectful enough to listen."

While he has been experimenting with finding his voice the last few years, he is still a natural listener, and it is a beautiful practice to witness. I often watch him, sometimes out the corner of my eye and watch the practice of the lost art of listening, in motion. It is like listening to poetry with no words, it seems to be this effortless dance of him listening intently, and when he does speak more often than not, it will be a question to the one, to whom he is listening.

Active listening is one of those practices that requires you to be fully in the moment with another, to be fully present with that person and their thoughts, views, and feelings. We have all been there, where we know we have not been listened to, we can instantly recognise when another is not fully present with us, or we are talked over the top of constantly. It is depleting, annoying, draining, and on the flip side, we also know how it feels when we have been there fully for another, and practiced the art of listening. It is rewarding, feels enriching, and we often come away, having learnt something.

I have noticed when I witness my husband listening to another, he is not only fully present, but he has no agenda, he is listening just to listen. He is listening to pay another the respect they deserve and I continue to learn from him daily, as I watch him practice this lost art with grace and humility.

You learn a lot when you listen. I am a natural talker, I am naturally shy, but I am naturally a talker. Yet my work asks me to listen. Demands that I listen, daily, minute to minute. I must also listen to what is *not being said.* My work, my way of life, would not make or have the impact it does if I did not.

Active listening requires focus, it takes patience, practice, and gets you down to the bare bones of your inner workings. The art of listening is deep inner work. The more you practice listening, the more it becomes obvious for you to know when to talk and when to be quiet and listen. You learn to listen to not only what is being said verbally, but also what is not being said. Taking it to a new level of 'listening' to another's body language, giving you new depths of insight.

To really listen requires you to be in, and *hold,* a sacred space for another. This builds relationships, which builds communities, which opens dialogue, creates respect and gradually expands out into the world where everyone begins to feel heard. Individuals become more present, and in the moment, which then in turn leads them to feeling less stress and anxiety.

When you master the art of listening to another, one of the pay offs and gifts is that, with practice, you learn to hold that space for yourself as well. When you hold that space for yourself and become fully in the moment, you create that moment in time to bring that art of listening to yourself and for yourself. You begin to dip your toes into the stillness inside, so you can then be in the position to listen to that quiet voice within. Not the voice of the head, which is the voice of judgement, fear, often lack of love, and conditioning, but the 'voice' of inner knowing, which is, Truth with a capital T. From this perspective you learn to make decisions from listening to the silence within, the peaceful, clear, and real place, not from listening to the chaotic noise from within, which is so often conditioned and imprinted in your mind.

Everybody has a point a view, everybody has a voice, no matter their education (formal or not), no matter where they come from, on what side of the tracks they have been raised, no matter how they appear. Everybody has a story, and a story of how they got to this moment in time. Everybody has experience in life no matter how short, and especially if it has been long. Everyone deserves the respect to be heard.

So, you see, mastering the art of listening ends up having many gifts which can keep giving, to not only others, but surprisingly for yourself as well.

When life comes along, and you have the strong urge to speak, take a moment, ask yourself, could this make an impact? Could what I want to say make a difference? Am I just speaking to speak? Do I find it difficult to simply listen?

And could you practice occasionally being the last to speak and see what happens and unfolds, it just may surprise you.

Seek to understand yourself.

Your Life is Not Falling Apart, You Are Cracking Open and Parts of You Are Falling Away

If you only take away one thing from this book, if you come back to only this knowledge, this knowing, when life comes along, it is this.........

Millions of small moments, and a few large stand out moments, micro, and macro, all connect to make and create your life.

Can your life change in a milli second? Absolutely.

Can your life take time to change? Absolutely.

When this moment comes along, because it will, take the time to momentarily explore, to really look at and take on board............ because change you do not plan, change you do not expect, you call problems, you call traumatic, you call un-nerving, it can feel like your life is falling apart. In fact, most would go so far as to say, "My life is falling apart!"

But if you take that moment, and look at it under a momentary magnifying glass, you may well realise it is not your life that is falling apart, parts of you are beginning to crack open, and *parts of you are falling away*. It is a part of yourself which *needs to die*, or has even *started dying*, so it can be re-born.

Once you come to this awareness, you realise your life is not a mess, *you* are a mess – energetically speaking. And when you are a mess energetically, life seems to follow.

**Remember…………….. equal and opposite reaction………
giant magnets……… and mirrors.**

Where you focus energy flows, and what you focus on
grows, whether you want it or not! There is a little but
very powerful practice in the next chapter where you can
experience this.

Once you are not only aware of being a mess energetically,
"Oh my god, I am a mess!" but are willing to clean yourself
up, 'energetically' speaking, your life will begin to turn
around. Absolutely.

It is as simple as that, do not over think it. You, we, me,
all can have the habit of complicating things, therefore
complicating life. When you decide to clean yourself up
energetically, your life will begin to turn around, and what
you focus on grows. Every time!

*The universe will align with your energy, not your words, so clean
up your act, and watch the law of attraction unfold soulfully.*

*Your life is not falling apart, parts of you are dying or maybe
already have, to make room for new growth, to make way for
new opportunities. You must fall apart; you must crack open to
become a new you.*

*You cannot build a new you on the foundation of the 'old you'
foundation. Let those parts of you shed, revealing clean, clear
energy. And life will change.*

Clean up your act and set your soul self free.

Where You Focus Energy Flows and What You Focus on Grows

Sit or lie in a comfortable position.

Take a few moments to connect with the breath.

As you consciously focus on your breath, your immediate environment will become less of a focus, and you will drop into your body.

You will still sense, hear, and be aware of what is around you, but your body will become your centre of attention.

Bring your awareness into your right ring finger. Breathe into your right ring finger, keep breathing into your right ring finger until you feel as though your finger lights up, or tingles, or feels warm, or expands, or feels light.

Bring your awareness into the whole of your right hand. Breathe into your right hand. Keep breathing into your right hand until your feel it 'light' up, tingle, feel warm or expand or even 'feel' light. You can feel all of these at the same time in your hand.

Breathe into the right forearm, elbow, top of the right arm, right shoulder. Keep breathing into the right arm until you feel it light up, tingle, feel warm, expand, or feel light.

Now *feel into* the difference between the rest of your body and the right arm.

Just for fun, now breathe into your left foot, focus your attention on your left foot, breathe into your left foot...............

Breathe into and focus on your left hand.................

Breathe into and focus on your low belly.................

Breathe into and focus on the whole of your left arm....................

Notice how these parts of the body *feel*. The energy shifts. the energy *feels* like it is shifting, opening, stimulating, energising, and igniting, simply by you shifting your focus.

You can feel into and move this potent energy all around your body. It is already there. It is part of you. You are made up of this precious and miraculous energy. But when you focus on it, it grows, and where you focus, the energy will flow. In your body and in life.

Focus on your bills, and it will feel as though all you seem to do, is pay bills.

Focus on your ailments, and it will feel you never experience reprieve, moving from one ailment to another.

Focus on gratitude and appreciation, and abundance in all areas will flow to you.

Focus on what works and is strong, fluid, agile in your body and you will feel more alive, and have more energy.

Whether it be wealth in peace or finance, vibrancy, abundance in time, or personal vigour, where we focus, the energy *will flow,* and what we focus on *will and does grow.*

Forgive Yourself

Forgive yourself for whatever haunts you.
For what keeps you up at night,
For what steels your thoughts.

Forgive yourself for what takes you away from your loved ones,
For what 'railroads' your mind away from lovemaking,
For what ushers you away from connecting with others.

Forgive yourself for what keeps the past in your present,
For what regurgitates the state of blame,
For what keeps your heart feeling strangled, heavy, or small.

Forgive yourself, it is the only way forward,
Forgive yourself, it is the only way to lighten the load.
Forgive yourself, it is the sacred compass to find your true north.
Forgive yourself, it is the only way to unchain the chambers of your heart,
It is the only way to live fully alive.

Forgive yourself, because it is not worth not doing that for yourself.
Forgive yourself for not being able to move on, but move forward,
Letting go of the past is not forgetting it, but honouring it,
Knowing the storms and tears through experiences have sculpted you into a fine piece of art, a one of a kind.
Knowing it has shaped you into a strong, empathetic, multifaceted, and wise you.

Forgive yourself, because if you don't, what will become of you?
Forgive yourself, as you deserve nothing short of peace,
You deserve a life lived in softness and strength,

care and courage,
wonder and wisdom,
and to become better not bitter.

Forgiveness, is the highest state of grace
Forgiveness, is the open gates to freedom
Forgiveness, because, it is all there is.

*Once you have the knowledge to move forward, then, **take** the action **required** to move forward!*

Stop Poisoning Your Well from Which You Drink

The longer you are on this planet, and in your 'Earth suit,' life comes right along with experiences of every sort, and your life either flails or deepens. Along comes as we know, joy, pain, fun, humour, love, loss, sadness, chaos, trauma, tranquillity, just to name a few.

Sadly, and all too often, when a traumatic experience or stressful event comes along, very rarely does one move through that situation with a mind conscious enough or open enough to know it is an opportunity to grow in some way. This is another life initiation. Rather, and unfortunately, unconsciously choosing to have a mind which rehashes the experience, time and time again, the individual then re-lives that trauma, sometimes for decades, with the mind and body reacting as if it is happening in that very moment.

The individual then goes to conventional therapy and talks *and talks and talks,* rehashing, regurgitating, repeating the constant "how does that make you feel?" For many, they remain in therapy for years, ending up on medication for years, sometimes decades with no clearer pathway to inner freedom. Often and sadly, finding only excuses as to why their life has panned out the way it has.

The thing is, our mind's job is not to make us happy, its job is to keep us safe. To keep us alive.

It is up to us, a decision in choice, which ends up being the most powerful thing we can do for ourselves.

Reflection, self-study, contemplation, observation and above all, sitting with and relaxing your heart is the beginning, the middle, and the end in practice, to clear the waters and keep them clean.

Becoming aware of your 'poison,' is the first step to 'clean the well from which you drink.' To open to life, where you have previously closed off. Put simply. Stop focusing on the past, and over thinking. Stop allowing past situations to interfere with your future.

When was the last time you simply sat with your heart?
Sit with your heart, now. Just sit.
Focus on your heart.
Feel your heart.
Relax your heart.
Feel the unclench .... Relax it more..........
Ahhhhhh .... There you go.

What we focus on matters.

What we feel matters.

What we think matters

What we focus on grows, and where we focus energy flows. Yoga taught me this.

What you feel must be felt until you 'outgrow' the feeling, until it no longer requires to be felt. Only then you can heal.

The stories you tell yourself sculpt your life, the stories you consistently tell yourself matter!

You can drag around the past in your present moment which really means you are *not* fully present, and in the moment. Your past 'soaked' present ends up poisoning your future. Let me ask you then, why on earth would you deliberately poison the well from which you drink?

Would you, knowing what you know, go and water your homegrown vegetable garden and fruit from a toxic well? One that is knowingly poisonous? Would you pick your produce, prepare it, and serve it up to your family? Would you knowingly build your home on a toxic waste site? Of course not!

So why then, are you *choosing* to live in the destructive poison of your 'past,' in your present moment? Why do you *choose* to live in past conversations, past hurts, past actions, past jealousy's, and past wrongs in your now? Do you want to feel how you are feeling for the next ten years? Next twenty years? Next thirty?

Even though you want to move it on, you no longer want to feel weighed down, you want to like the person you are, you know it is not serving you……. Or is it?

Has it been serving you? Yes, in a way. With chronic stress, anxiety, depression, there is a payoff. Always a payoff. Remember, your brain is there to keep you alive, not happy. Its purpose is to protect you. The stories you tell yourself can either get you through, to just survive, or to blossom and thrive.

Your thoughts can either kill you or heal you. Your anger, blame, hatred, or shame can become masks that you wear, or a false sense of strength which can administer venom to those around you in not only words but actions. This poison, isn't just passed out to others, the noxious residue of your thoughts imbed themselves in everything you do. The stories you tell yourself can either be an excuse as to why your life is the way it is, why your unfit body is the way it is, why your health is the way it is, why your finances are the way they are, why your wife cheated on you, why your husband left you, why you lost your job, it could go on........

Or

You can use your past, your challenges, your trauma, to teach yourself, and others. The opportunities to learn deeply about yourself, are endless.

The gifts in becoming the ultimate bullshit detector, to be able to 'sense' another's true character, even when they are presenting the opposite in public or personally to you. To be able to have the "I get knocked down, but I get up again, you aint ever gonna keep me down" attitude, to "I will never give up." The gift of becoming the most loving husband or wife, to being an 'in tune' parent, to not only having an intuitive wisdom but the deepest of deep wisdom, we can *only* gain through tough life experience. By not dwelling, but in reflection.

These are gifts which keep on giving, strengthening your resolve, and forever deepening your insights.

To be a beacon of towering light for others, a safe harbour for others who need to weather and rest from their own storms. To become an example, that trauma *is what you experienced it is not who you are,* it does not have to wear you down but rather, it can shape you, and to pass on, that others too have a choice.

1. *Focus on where you want to go, not where you have been. Focus on the body to rest the mind.*
2. *To feel the feeling until you beautifully outgrow it and the feeling is no longer required to be felt. As you mature and grow spiritually you come to outgrow many of the things you once deemed impossible to surrender.*
3. *FOCUS ON THE BODY SO YOU REST THE MIND. Concentrate, and follow the breath. Feel your feet on the ground, feel your hands. Sit quietly with your heart.*
4. *Choose to change the story you tell yourself.*

And .... relax the heart,
Relax the heart
Relax the heart.

"Both poverty and riches are the offspring of thought."

Napoleon IIill

When Life Came Along

Life comes along in many ways, slowly but surely at times, and others, you are catapulted into navigating an extreme situation or experience.

Life came along for me at the very young age of six, it hurled me into a childhood different to many others.

When the groping started, at first over my dress or over my cord pants, it was very much a thought, "did that just happen?" along with the feeling of embarrassment and awkwardness. And so began the years of him bringing his fingers to his lips creating the signal to, "shhhhh."

As he gained confidence, I think, the signal to "shhhhh" was followed with a deliberate pull down of my pants and the slow undoing of his top button and click by click of his zip. The warm white snotty like consistency stuck to my low belly. He would flick it off, then wipe the residue away with almost a caring way about him.

"It's natural that we do this." He would whisper while not looking at me. I was eight.

I was scared, not the scared way of my life being under threat, but the scared as in feeling ashamed of telling my parents. I knew he should not have been doing this to me, it felt so wrong, I felt wrong, and everything felt wrong within me, so of course, I wanted to tell my parents. So many times, I really did, but could not find the words out loud. It was like one of those nightmare dreams where you go to scream, but nothing comes out. I would even start the sentence silently in my head, and in my mind's eye I would play out the scene of what my parents would say and do. Even in my pretend scene of playing out the telling of what was going on, they never not believed me. But I did not tell them.

I will call him T. With T's needs mounting confidence, I guess, the "shhhhhh" came first, then the sound of his zip slowly undoing his jeans. He climbed on top of me still with his finger to his lips signalling me to "shhhhhh." Penetration snapped my eyes wide open with the sting and burn. Even my tears which welled but refused to fall seemed to have a sting about them. He always finished off on my belly, then wiping away the disgusting warm white snot like jelly, or he would catch as much as he could in his hand. If we were outside 'hiding me' behind some stone building, or fence, he would flick it out into the long grass.

I was ten.

In desperation and wanting it to stop, embarrassment and shame taking over, I played out the scenario of the conversation I so desperately wanted to have with my Mum. Yet a crippling fear always smothered me like the heavy cloak of darkness. To me, my Dad was the hero, my hero. To me, the fierce protector of his family.

My Dad would protect his family at all costs or go down fighting. He was proficient in martial arts and also taught. I do not know whether I overheard it, he said it to me, or the love was so deep for us, he let us know, that if anyone else ever hurt us in any way, he would kill them. I took it seriously and literally, even though wise beyond my years at that age, still in my age-old mind in that time, I took what my Dad said to be completely and utterly true.

I would go to bed at night with visions, if I told them what was happening to me, I would be visiting him in jail. I genuinely felt that would become my reality.

When the cars left the house, where we were visiting, leaving me with T, he had no need to "shhhhhhh" me. No one would hear me anyway. He led me to the bathroom, with my heart pumping so hard it was going to burst out my chest. The apprehension and knowing what was going to happen next, the fear froze my legs, my voice, and my logical thinking.

He unzipped my jeans, then slowly his. The sound of the teeth in the zip, calculated, and smooth with every click. I can still hear in the echo of the bathroom. The force of entry. The sting, the burn. I know he was not fully in, deep, as I was small and tight due to my age and being a gymnast, but enough to hurt, and burn, even hours afterward. I was frozen stiff, my head turned harshly to one side and my eyes clenched shut.

As he gained an awkward rhythm, probably due to listening for my Mum's car in the driveway, he always kept his pants on, I am sure so he could hurriedly make his escape. "Move! You need to move! Open your legs! This is natural. The pain will ease, it always hurts at first." Frustrated and angry, he pulled out and finished himself off over the bathroom floor. I remember him cleaning himself up over the hand basin.

"Don't tell anyone, you can never tell anyone."

I slowly peeled myself off the bathroom floor. Sore, embarrassed. Adjusting my clothes. I left to watch TV in the loungeroom. Luney Tunes. When my Mum arrived back, all looked normal. I was crying inside.

This was one of the most painful times, physically and emotionally, with the most deliberate focus on T's part. His look had changed, his manner had changed. Things were changing, he was starting to use the strength of his mind games. My fear came to bed with me, ate with me, went to school with me, sat with me while I did my homework. I felt people could see what had happened to me, on my face, in my walk, in my school work. But no one ever inquired. I was eleven.

I broached the conversation as I was worried, felt sick to my stomach with the what if's. I quizzed my Mum about the birds and the bees. Secretly hoping she would pick up on my questions and ask if everything was alright. I scooted around the conversation for a while not wanting to bring a suspicion to my words. And yet at the same time I wanted her to save me. "She was not getting it! Oh my God!" She was simply just answering my questions. I still remember as I write this, the feeling of screaming inside. My eleven-year-old insides were screaming a blood curdling desperate scream but only silence passed my lips. In the end, I blurted out "What if, for an example, if someone T's age, and someone my age had sex, could I have a baby?"

"No darling, you must be old enough, gone through puberty to be able to get pregnant." She went on to beautifully explain as she had the ability to do on any subject, in detail what needed to happen.

That was the only clue I ever tried to drop. It was not their fault, and as a parent myself now, would I have known? And before you ask, "How could they have not known?" Well, I developed a skill set of that of a seasoned actress. I practiced and performed daily, unknowingly honing in on a skill set that was needed to survive. I often lived in the world of 'make believe' when I was in my own company, even well into young adulthood. Spending time in this 'make believe' world gave me the reprieve from my own mind, to live another day. To be able to 'change' an ending in my own mind from what had either just happened, or as an adult lost in memories from when I was seven, nine or eleven years of age, whether it was in the physical or in conversation was a saviour.

In the thousands of 'make believe' conversations with my parents, they never not believed me, they comforted me, protected me, helped me heal, and fought for me. In my imaginary world I plotted revenge, raged war, 007 sort of stuff, way out there, sometimes even inserting myself in movie scenes, undercover, not only fighting and planning the ultimate punishment for my wrongdoer, but with the soul intention of raging a war in purification of anyone like that on the planet. This enabled me to 'escape' not only as a child, but as a young woman.

So no, they did not know, how could they? I became undeniably and sadly, a brilliant actress.

I was practicing on our piano, T made his way toward me. It felt more deliberate, more rushed, the approach scarier than before, it had a more desperate feel about it; was it him or me feeling desperate? It was as if he was already short on time, to get 'it done' before he was caught? Grabbing the top of my arm forcefully, he pulled at me, my hands slid off the keys, I jumped up, and pulled back.

"No!"

T's finger raised to his lips, "shhhhhhh...."

"NO!" I still feel the power of not only my glare, but of that little two letter word. Never had I been witness to, heard, or spoken, in the lowest of calculated tone of voice; and been so epically powerful.

In that moment my life changed .... yet again.

He tried, but he never touched me again. **It was done.**

He was well known to my family as so often is the case. He was trusted. And being known to our family, of course, we saw him often and continued to do so. Remembering my parents knew nothing.

He stole from me, he violated me, he hurt me, sometimes there would be only a week between the disturbing experience, occasionally there would be a month reprieve between, of what was to become a harrowing time. Regularly repetitive for years.

When life comes along, and in a hundredth of a milli second, you get the cellular guts, knowhow, and courage to change something, you take that moment with everything you have. Every fibre of your being is guiding you, leading you, moving you, and fighting for you. The soul part of you which is eternal, backs you and guides you, every inch of the way, even in the youngest years of age.

I look back now and that "NO!" had untold power behind it. It had all the "No's" of every single girl and woman in the world who couldn't muster up the ability, courage, physical strength or know how, to say no. It had the magnified power of every girl and woman who has said "No" and taken back their power to make change, from the longest time in history, to the recent past, and in our present time.

As I reflect, and write these words, I come to realize that, that "No" was not just mine, it was a collective "NO." Two letters, to create the smallest of words, that can have one of the greatest impacts in a person's life.

Years of abuse, assault, rape, force, coercion, silence, secrets .... was done. It was over.

When life comes along, it can be in the form of a traumatic experience, hardship, heart ache, betrayal, or loss.

So, what do you do now?

What do you do when you feel your world has been shattered, the rug pulled out from underneath you? Where everything you have ever believed in does not seem to exist. Where you would rather live in the disillusion of your mind's conversation, than in the realness of memories in what happened. Where at the same time, the rehashing of the memory is on repeat in your mind, where long after the physical act has passed, the suffering is experienced in the body as if it is still happening.

What *do* you do?
You Rebuild……………..

It is important to remember
who you were
before the trauma.

Your Body Keeps Score

One day, it will become normal for conventional medicine to take the 'holistic approach,' to treat the individual 'as a whole,' and not segregate mind from body and vice versa. One day......... body, mind, and spirit together, will be treated with the reverence they deserve. As one; because they are.

Two quotes, by different physicians more than one hundred years ago.

"The sorrow which has no vent in tears may make other organs weep."
Dr Henry Maudsley 1895

And

"The organ weeps the tears the eyes refuse to shed."
Sir William Osler 18th Century physician

The Foundation for Rebuilding

These Physicians were aware of how powerful the mind is and intelligent the body is, and together a real powerhouse. Just as the Yogis for thousands of years and the ancient sages too, have known this to be true, the Ayurvedic Doctors, and approach, one of the oldest and wisest medicine and treatments; treat the individual *as a whole* person, including the spirit of that individual.

Sadly, in conventional medicine, there are few doctors who delve into the cause of 'dis-ease.' Much of this system only treats the symptoms. And what have you noticed? We are getting sicker as a society. Poor health and obesity run rampant. Our children appear to be more messed up than ever before. Our teenagers do not know whether they, as my grandmother used to say about herself, "I don't know whether I am Arthur or Martha today." Self -harm, anxiety, depression appears to be evident in children as young as six or seven years of age. ***This is not natural!***

As a society in our adulthood and teenage years, all we seem to talk about is mental health. It is at the forefront in adverts, on television, in the news, social media, magazines, governments, and the medical system, and just like so many children, we are getting sicker, physically, emotionally, mentally, and spiritually. The more we talk about it, the worse it gets.

Firstly, we are coming at it from the wrong angle, treating only the symptoms.

Secondly, have you ever wondered, really wondered, *do the medical systems and drug companies really want us to be a healthy world?* To be healthy people and communities? You think how ill health in any form has become a multi-trillion-dollar industry. My question is, "Are we really focused on healthy minds, bodies, and lives?"

What we focus on grows and where we focus energy flows. When we look at depression or anxiety for example, what story we tell ourselves daily, become the cues and then the foundation, for our emotional and mental health. If you keep living in the past, if you do not resolve or learn from, or move on from, and change the old story of the past trauma or pain, your thoughts keep relaying to your body that the past event is still happening now. It literally keeps the trauma circulating and pumping around your body. It keeps it alive. Not only on a mental and emotional level, but a physical one as well.

It may even settle in the body taking up residence in an organ, bone, or some part of the body which connects, responds, and reacts to the story you have kept alive. The trauma you have experienced when left unattended, buried deep within, or been allowed to be relived daily, can manifest in your body as a very physical symptom.

If you could only look inside your body and really see what the elevated and relentless drip and release of the stress hormone cortisol does in your body, not to mention adrenaline, and norepinephrine, exhausting your adrenals, you would never allow it to happen. They are designed to help us with immediate stressful situations. Fight, flight, or freeze. When they go into protection mode, these hormones increase your heart rate, blood sugar levels, and blood pressure. Stress hormones, however, which **never** get a chance to turn off, rather than only turning on when needed, create havoc with your system. From weight gain, to stress headaches, depression, anxiety, increased sugar also known as glucose in the blood stream, diabetes, obesity, insomnia, thyroid disfunction, just to name a few.

A dripping tap can erode a foundation…………..

When the stress hormones continue to course through the body, the body reacts as if the past is being lived in the present. I, myself experienced this for years; waking in the middle of the night with pulse racing, sweating, shaking, headaches, and chronic muscle tension so severe, it felt as though my whole body had 'lock jaw.' My past was being experienced as my 'now' moment; even in my sleep! And so powerful, even waking me up! This means your body never gets a chance to just simmer down and relax fully, it remains on guard, hyper alert, ready for danger, ready to run, to fight, or to hide. We can then suffer with anything from muscle tension and fatigue, digestive issues, sleep challenges, sleep disturbances, headaches, PTSD, autoimmune challenges, depression, just to name a few more. Is this you?

When your body stays on high alert, the past remains in your body, your thoughts create the story. *Your story.* The story you tell, the story you live, keeps the past alive and well, and your body suffering, is living the 'victim life.'

It is here in this place; you *continue* to live the victim life. Never going beyond your suffering. Never courageous enough to look beyond what you have come to live daily. From this perspective, we blame another for our life, we can come to rely on medications, even if our medication is alcohol, hoping it will take the pain away, hoping it will enable us to sleep, hoping it will elevate our mood, hoping it will relieve habitual tension, hoping it will erase painful memories. It is not unusual for people to spend years in 'talking' therapy, dissecting their stories, rehashing, and the regurgitation "how does that make you feel?"

When the body is already on high alert, we are *just existing,* in a daily dose of fight, flight, or freeze, and at times even fawn; rehashing, it only keeps it alive, holding the stress in the body.

If you want to rebuild your life..................

Firstly, *you must feel, then you can heal.* We will expand on this in the next few pages, *First You Must FEEL, Only Then, Can You Heal.*

Secondly, you must change your perspective on your past. You must learn to look at it differently, because if you do not, your body will take it on board, and it will store it in the deepest layers of your core. It is time to reframe the story you have been telling, if you don't, your past stories will continue to consume you. Poisoning that well, from which you drink, in this present moment and certainly for your future.

Anti-depressants can be handed out like lollies, rather than them being temporary during the acute phase, where sometimes they can be of benefit, sadly, and all too often, the individual, may stay on them for years, even decades.

You will never move through depression, or on from hidden stress, headaches, or underlying pain, unless you first *acknowledge your pain, and the story you have been telling yourself, with an open inquiring heart.*

No anti-depressant, no pill, no medications will heal you. Trust me, I know.

You must dig deep, you must honour, you must get honest, you must get curious, **and you must be WILLING to move forward.**

No one outside of yourself can heal you, or put back together the parts of you that *feel* broken.

They can assist you, but this, you must decide to do yourself. So, if your body appears to be failing you, it is not. If your body appears to be old beyond your years, it is not, if your body is not how you want it, then change something. Do something different.

If not, your body will store your past, your trauma and your pain into everyday niggles, everyday discomfort, to ongoing fatigue, autoimmune challenges and more. Instead, could you ask yourself, "What can this teach me?"

You can if you are willing, and open; allow the past, any trauma or pain to teach you, strengthen you, build you, and direct you, to enhance your life.

You are strong, you have already survived, you are here! Reading these words.

Now....... don't you want to thrive?

'Rebuilding'

Your thoughts are like tugboats. Have you ever thought how on earth given its size, can a tugboat shift a ship, tow it, push it, nudge it, and manoeuvre it the way it does? It is fascinating to watch.

Your thoughts may not seem like much, as you think all day, the words you speak may not seem significant, *but, eventually, you speak your thoughts, you live your thoughts, and they become a belief system. Which become your life. You think it, you become it.* Your thoughts may seem random, but they are not. Thoughts are not random, and thoughts ooze out of you and most are repetitive.

Your thoughts have tremendous power behind them, just like the metaphorical tugboat.

When you physically compare a tugboat to an enormous ship, you do wonder how on earth this small, insignificantly sized, little boat can tow, nudge, push and shift an enormous monstrosity of a ship, with such precision. I do anyway! But it does.

Your thoughts are the same as the tugboat. Seemingly insignificant most of the time, benign, but ………. if left unchecked, and allowed to go on their merry way unconsciously, eventually your thoughts will push you around, lead you astray, keep you supressed, freeze you in your tracks and keep you small. If your mind has been running the show, then it is time you befriend your mind. And eventually master your mind. Aren't you tired of your mind running the show and enslaving you within your everyday?

Would you like your mind to work for you instead? Because it can. *If I can get my mind to work for me for the most part, you can do this for yourself too.* I am no different to you. The question to ask yourself, "What am I towing behind my tugboat? What could I move out of my way and clear the path for?"

In other words, what you think will either push back against you or drag along behind you, which ends up being your life. In essence, your thoughts become your life. I have been there, so I understand.

Become more mindful in the power of your thoughts.

This is the first step to re-building. I understand you may have suffered, but if you keep thinking it, you will keep living it. Your past experiences, if you allow them, will wake up with you, dine with you, go out with you, drive with you. Your body will experience it as if it is still happening. You end up having a visceral response, and your body is traumatised all over again, day in day out, month in month out, and years get swallowed up by depression, anxiety, stress, or insomnia, and eventually 'dis-ease' in the body.

You think and you manifest, no matter what it is, whether you want it or not.
You think your thoughts and your body responds.
You think your thoughts and the world responds.

So now choose………… it is after all your choice.
Choose to ask better questions about your position.
Choose to think a better thought.
Becoming mindful of your thoughts is setting the foundation
for you to rebuild.

Instead of asking "why did this happen to me?"
Or "why does this keep happening to me?"
Ask instead,
"What did I get from it?"
"What do I still get from it?"
"What is the payoff?"
"What have I learnt from it?"
"What knowledge have I gained?"
"What hidden gifts do I now possess?"
"What gifts have I received?"

Begin to make friends with your mind, then learn to master
it. Allow it to become an asset for you, so you can steer it in
the right direction for yourself, where you can utilise it and
benefit, rather than it using you.

You are the master of your mind. So, master it!

First You Must Feel, Only Then, Can You Heal

There is a discomfort in looking into the shadow self in the Western World. We shun it, refuse to look at it, or more often than not, gloss over it, and even deny it is a real thing.

The shadow self is the part of you that lies beneath the social mask you wear daily. It is the part of yourself which is trauma infused, sad, the part which feels wounded, the part which is only ever okay if the world and those around us behave a certain way, it is the part that we do not allow anyone else to see.

The shadow or darker part of yourself is not easy to look at or feel. It is the of part you, you are often so desperately trying to hide from the world, and more importantly hide from yourself. It can feel frightening. It was certainly the part of me I did not want to look at, even though back then I had no words for this shadow self. I knew it was something I had to go to and visit with a conscious awareness if I was to heal certain aspects of my life.

We often deny this part of ourselves, and avoid looking close into any direction where by it might lead us. **However,** *if you are desiring and wanting change in your life, it is time to get uncomfortable for a short time to uncover the treasures and gifts, rather than being uncomfortable for a life time.*

1. **Notice how your body feels right now.**

How is your body taking in your environment? Right now, at this very moment? Do you know?

Can you feel it? ***Do you even know?*** Where are you feeling tension?

Sit with this question for a conscious moment .... where are you *feeling* tension?

Most of us do not even take the moments in our day to ask "how is my body feeling right now?" In this moment.

It is my experience in working with individuals from all walks of life, from all over the world, so many do not take the time to befriend their body. If only we were taught in school to learn to body scan, to learn to know where our stress, trauma, or anxiety, is residing in our body.

It is from this awareness, that you can learn to read, *feel,* and honour your body in real time, as your outward environment feels as though it alters your inner environment.

When you can learn this, you are now learning to befriend your body. Every memory of stress or trauma reacts in the body, every emotion reacts in the body. Learn to assess the body in any given moment. **Any given moment.**

This practice teaches you the language of the body.

2. **Relax.**

"Relax?" I hear you say! "How can I relax when I have all *this* going on? How can I relax when I lived through a traumatic experience? How can I relax when I am struggling daily? How can I relax when I am stressed to the eyeballs?"

Learn to relax. I spoke about this in my first book *Rising with the Phoenix*. Relaxing is not just for the couch, or for when you are on holidays, or when you are practicing yoga, or meditating. ***Relaxation is something we can learn, in fact, it is something we must learn.***

You can learn to relax while taking an exam, doing the dishes, public speaking, taking a meeting, cooking dinner. Discomfort, habitual tension if unchecked, can turn into physical pain in the body. ***Your body when in the state of 'dis-ease' is begging you to take notice, begging you to release your trauma, begging you to release your stress, begging you to take care of it emotionally.***

When my body 'failed me,' when I was in my late thirties, it was actually 'waking' me up. It was begging me for some emotional care. I was to learn, I must admit, the painstaking way to learn the language of my body, to learn to befriend my body, and to learn and teach my mind that it now must work for me, not me work for it.

It was uncomfortable, highly uncomfortable, and with every layer I peeled back, and if I refused to peel it back myself, it was peeled back for me, to layers of disturbance, to layers of unrest, it became an archaeological uncovering of trauma after trauma, stress after stress, wound after wound, habit after habit.

There was an unlearning of habitual 'so called' knowingness and a learning of the wisest wisdom. I needed to learn to relax into the pain, learn to relax in the suffering. To go beyond the mind, and drop fully into my body.

Pain is so painful, I fully understand. The mind and body are so brilliant, the inner intelligence of both, so magnificently precise. So specifically designed. They will do everything they can to get you through the day, the week, and the year. They help keep you safe. 'Shielding' you from other 'onslaughts' from life, protecting you from more harm. Whether it be damaging and detrimental in the long run or not, they will keep you safe.

What it comes down to, however, what we are really wanting and needing, is long term sustainability in wellness, emotionally, physically, mentally, and of course, spiritually.

Relaxing asks you to listen to your body, witness your mind, so you can find more peace, more ease in different moments in your days, and with practice you will gradually learn to, often, not always, but often, step into your own empowerment.

Empowerment within your own mind and body will enable you to become more self-reliant, more resilient. So, when triggers do present themselves because they will when life comes along, they will no longer rock your world, but become more subtle in your response system, your physical system, your whole self.

Learning to relax in any given moment can be difficult and almost seen as impossible. But I am here to say it is possible and not only possible, it is necessary to move toward healing yourself and your life. To come back to your true self. Your whole self.

Living in a sense of agitation, anger, depression, anxiousness, insomnia, muscular tension, is not your true self. They are not your natural state of being. Through habit, it is who you *think* you have become.

Your true self is peaceful, balanced, joyful, harmonious. Now let us just clarify, you will not live in peace and harmony all the time, you will not live a Zen existence day in day out, but you will live peacefully as frequently as you can.

You will wobble, but the wobble will not become a month-long mood, blame period, or another belief system in the making. You will come back to peace, abundance, and harmony more and more, until they become you, and you come back to the natural state of them.

I heard once, "you are not responsible for what happened to you, but you are responsible for what you are going to do with it." I love this, and it is true!

It is up to you! It is and always will be up to you!

At first anything takes effort to do, but over time, and with a belief system shift, it is who you become.

The Power of Rage

When life comes along, it *always* presents an opportunity to move into a healing space, to practice forgiveness.

Forgiveness is one of the main ingredients to coming back to a state of wholeness, oneness, *and maintaining* that state of oneness and wholeness. To coming back to your true self, complete self, time and time again.

When working with an individual, I have heard them say, "I have forgiven." "I've dealt with that." "I've let that go." "I know that," with an almost robotic, persuasive, and rehearsed line. Trying to convince themselves more than me most likely, but not only does their body tell me a different story, the energy they radiate outward, does not match the words with which they are trying to convince me, but more importantly, themselves.

I get it. I so get it! I was once there too. And to be perfectly honest, not so long ago, this interestingly enough, reared its head. However, with the practices which have become part of my life, I was able to really feel, listen and watch with a certain detachment. My practice of forgiveness and living in alignment has well and truly, *and* beautifully been entrenched in my life for many years now. So, I was fascinated for this to take place for myself, even after all these years.

This is very common in individuals I work with, when they begin their road to seriously practice forgiveness and bring it into their life, to move forward, and set themselves free.

There is a part of them which thinks, "I am forgiving now, I am choosing the path of forgiveness, so I must not be angry or feel anger. I must not have outrage in my body, or in my mind. Think positively, I must be positive."

But ....

At that stage within my daily practices which have simply become a part of me, I could no longer imagine, not having these practices and awarenesses in my life. What began to show up interestingly, was that whenever I sat in silence, or became mindful of my thoughts, and for a long-time mind you, looking back, I think it was there! And during this time even when I meditated, all I could hear, even though it was barely audible, I had to listen with *all* my senses, was an inner scream.

My silence, on the surface, was quiet, it seemed, silent. But when I really felt into the silence, and listened, almost beyond my human ears, the silence was filled with a whispering scream! "Oh my God!" I tried to push it away, tried to deny it, rationalise it, "This cannot be!" "How can this be?" I tried to hush it, tried not to hear it, but inside I was screaming. Really screaming. A blood curdling scream, yet .... silent.

And as I continued to either ignore it, or talk to myself, "this cannot *really* be there, can it?" It got to the point, even as I stacked the dishwasher, sat at the beach, read a book, went for a walk, or run, deep internally beyond my ears, was the inner scream.

Deep beyond my love, my teaching, my every day, my everything, was rage. An invisible, silent rage. I didn't even realise it was there! Rage was haemorrhaging from my beingness. Rage was blocking me from taking a full breath, it was behind my smile, it was screaming while I read a novel, it tucked me in at night. Whenever I got quiet, all I could hear was a scream. It was unmistakable. The scream which had no sound, filled every chasm within my physical body.

In yoga we call this a Samskara. Samskara is a Sanskrit word meaning 'impression' and it is said to be, and I have found this to be the case, the most important and powerful impact influencing our life.

A Samskara is a blockage within you, literally an impression from your past. It is a mental impression, a psychological imprint within your body and mind. A samskara or emotional wound, from a traumatic event, stress, or moment which has never been fully dealt with, in other words, it is unfinished business.

Unfortunately, this blockage, impression, or undercurrent, often ends up running your life. Without you even knowing it!

Samskaras, blockages, or impressions, particularly from a traumatic event or experience, do not just disappear on their own. When we hold on to past hurts, or trauma, our energetic flow becomes blocked, *because we block it!* From this place and perspective, life no longer flows through us, it feels like it no longer flows for us, we come up against road blocks, difficulties, we feel as though things are always hard, that we are always pushing. We get tired more easily, day to day events rock us more easily. Or maybe things never turn out, we can either end up fixating on the same thoughts and stressful language and patterns, or we can unknowingly feel stuck, depressed, anxious with no evident way out.

This is commonly known as 'GETTING IN YOUR OWN WAY.'

These impressions, can keep you feeling blocked, and stuck for sometimes decades, and when this happens, you end up closing off your heart. It hardens, you lose the ability to be able to listen to and follow your gut feeling. You are now closed down, and closed off.

This was me for a long time. Is this you? Where life has come along and rather than you putting it down to a life lesson, or an opportunity for new growth, *you have, on some level decided to hold onto it, thereby stifling your flow, blocking you from receiving the abundance, peace, and harmony in so many areas of your life.*

While I, at that point in time, did not feel fully shut down, I felt for the most part clear, and more centred than off centre, however, in my quietest of moments, there was something which was disturbing the quiet. In my quietest of moments, I was silently screaming.

This inner scream came from a place in me so deep, it felt too far away, too foreign to even comprehend; a chasm so deep it was undetected and undiscovered by me up until now. Obviously over the years, I had peeled enough layers off my emotional onion to a place where this scream could now be heard. Just! But to say it was obvious once I heard it, was an understatement to say the least. You cannot unsee something, and you certainly cannot unhear something.

This had my full undivided attention.

In what felt to be knee deep in and completely immersed in the practising of forgiveness, and even deeper in the feelings of what I had forgiven, where it felt to now be a part of my every day, was this hair-raising silent scream.

And then there it was, unexpectedly and dubiously, I was welcoming another layer of forgiveness. Of awareness. Remembering sometimes forgiveness, is about forgiving yourself, it is not always about another.

In what I could only call Grace. Grace created just enough space for forgiveness to open yet another door, which appeared to be multi-layered, and multi-dimensional, it was more open, deeper, vast, and to what felt like the grass roots, down into the epicentre of it all, to what I had been practicing and immersing myself in, but now with absolutely no force, it was, genuinely, cellularly felt.

Behind the door which grace so delicately opened for me, to which I tentatively opened wider, was rage. Rage was at my epicentre which grace so lovingly opened for me, forgiveness led me by the hand to meet rage openly and with intent.

And rage I did.

Over a period of days, I let loose with swearing, screaming, yelling. I took the axe and chopped logs. I destroyed old furniture, I smashed old plates into a skip bin, I took heavy metal music to its limit in volume, lifting the roof off our home, and after a whirlwind of deliberateness that felt sooooooo good, so liberating, and with no judgement, the scream was gone. She fell silent. And when I peeked within, the silence wore the softest of smiles.

Sometimes you cannot have forgiveness without rage. You could never plant a crop on toxic waste land and expect a healthy yield in which you would feel comfortable consuming. *You cannot fully experience forgiveness if there is rage bubbling underneath the surface.*

So, listen, listen deep, listen with openness, listen with your subtlest of senses, listen with your 'beyond human' ears, and do not be afraid to rage.

Finish your business.

Let the end, the finish, be the magnificent beginning.

Let everything you have stored so deep, where you have basement after basement of negative storage, detrimental blockages, finally move through you, and then out.

Feel your heart open, so life can flow toward you and through you once again. You will in that split second, and with awareness, become more present, *and* more in the moment than you have ever been. And when life comes along again, rather than just thinking you have dealt with a situation or you think you have forgiven another, *you will now feel it, know it, and therefore become it.*

So, rage, let go, forgive, and find flow.

There is no end point
to healing,
we are in a constant state
of transformation.

Little by little, as you
find yourself,
you free yourself.

*You will get to a point where you are no longer
interested in band-aids,*

*you will find the root cause to disturbances
and suffering.*

And you will happily dig that

sucker out!

Out of the Black Hole

There is great power when we take the time to learn the skills needed, to understand stress and trauma. Really understand it. Not just *think* we do, but really come to *know* it.

Take the time to delve into getting to know your preconceived ideas and notions of how the world should be, *according to you*. How things should be and look, and how much you grab hold of that notion, to control it and manipulate it; to make sure it is a certain way so you will be alright. When you take a moment to observe this........ You are *then* on track to freedom, to peace and to learning about your best higher self. So, the question becomes, *what do you have to do, who do you have to become to access the higher self-version of you?*

When you are manipulating things to be a certain way, so you will feel safe and be okay, *you are relying on the outside world to be okay, then you will never be okay.* This is not living a joyous life, and certainly not a calm one. If you are relying on the outside world to be okay, then you will find yourself always on guard, always on alert, and always in some form of unrest.

This way of being, to always be on alert is a form of *only existing,* it is tedious, frustrating, and exhausting. When you arrive at this point of awareness, it is a serious rising out of the ashes. This is the beginning of the spiritual awakening. *When you no longer blame or expect the world to be a certain way, but ask yourself, "How have I contributed to this? How have I contributed to my life becoming ……… tired?" "How have I dug my own 'hole,' and how long was I digging?* "You come to realise in an instant, digging yourself out of the black hole, out from rock bottom, is not only a mental process, but also an engaging of the body. After years of shutting down, shutting off, closing down, and closing off, your whole nervous system *will* need a full restoration.

This can take time, but it does not have to. It can take months; it may take a few years. But it does not have to. I hear you say "oh my God, two to three years? Of more work? That is too hard! I do not think I can do that, that is too much like hard work!"

And now I ask *you*…… "Really? Harder than the ten years? Twenty years? Forty decades of pain and feeling bloody awful, of not reaching your goals? Of not living a calm and curious life? Of numbing yourself with everything from social media, television, alcohol, drugs, or as a workaholic? Or living Groundhog Day? Or not allowing yourself to be fully accessible and open with your partner, your children, your friends, your life?"

It does not take extra time. *This work does not take you away from your life. It is your life!* You meld it into your every day. It is not an extra task to be done on top of everything else. It can take just a few minutes of conscious awareness daily, to change your life. You can connect to your breath while doing the dishes, you can sit with your heart as a passenger in a car, or your breath, for even just 5 minutes a day. Five minutes a day!

Just five minutes a day starts to change the neuro pathways in your brain, changes the way your body physiologically responds to certain situations in your day. This is how change, positive change begins to alter your way of being, in monumental ways. Your energy will start to change. The blockages will start to clear and find their way out of your body and 'being-ness.' You will break negative habits and break the cycle of habitual stress, emotional pain, and trauma.

Isn't it time to stop allowing your past stories, your past impressions, samskaras, to fuel and fertilise your suffering, the stresses, the turmoil, and the strain, or even just the 'ho hum' which has become your life?

Remember, in my last book, Heal the Whole Woman, a thought is just a thought until you give it meaning. You no longer need to buy into these outdated, stress and habitually filled, trauma fuelled thoughts, even if not that dramatic, maybe simply humdrum stories, which *you have allowed* to block you.

Isn't it tiring coming up against resistance all the time? It is the resistance to something which causes so much angst, so much anxiety, so many sleepless nights, the knot in your stomach.

Acceptance is the antidote to resistance. If we do not accept where we are at this moment, if we do not accept the uphill battle within, if we do not accept the truth, the *real* truth, which we have been denying up until now, then we will continue to resist.

And when we live in a constant state of resistance, there is always dramatisation attached to this 'lifestyle.' When you add in your drama to a situation which, you are also resisting, the cycle will inevitably continue.

As you come to practice acceptance, you will find as circumstances arise, you will face a situation with clarity, just as it is being presented to you, without your stories circulating around it, without your own drama, fear, and the need to control the outcome.

You will allow things to unfold and respond accordingly, not react from a place of your past traumas, habits, and pain, from your old story. And guess what, you will then drop into the present moment, without personal bias. Without your personal taste becoming involved. Without the need to control. The world around you then, will not trigger your pain point, and send you regressing back to the past.

You will become consciously aware of the moment unfolding before you. It will flow through you with no more blockages layering on top of each other within you. In yoga we become acutely aware that there is no other moment that exists, except the moment in which you find yourself. When you are aware of being in the present moment, *everything* opens when you are in that moment. *Everything.* Your heart, your mind, and your senses. *There is no dragging the past into pollute this moment, and there is no future with concern to tighten your belly. Just the moment you are in. It is as simple as that.*

It is in this space you let go of yourself, you get out of your own way. You *are* capable of this. And with practice you will become *more* than capable of being in the moment. Any given moment. Free of anxieties, of fearful stories and of blocked energy. You become free to live in the moment, *this* moment. Because that is all there is.

You are *now* free to be open, if you so *choose*.

It is up to you.

Rebuilding is Simple But it is Not Easy

You have been given the gift of many moments, which string, melt, and meld, fusing together, to create this wondrous life of yours, and in this blending, and intertwining, many events take place.

We are all here for such a short time, it feels like forever in one breathe and just a moment in time in another. Between your birth and death is a wonderous and unique experience, individual to you.

Would you choose, consciously choose, to really live out your time between your birth and your death, with a stress filled and tension filled existence, from fabricated, to embellished stories, from which you believe to be true, to which you have been *and* become a major contributor?

Just relax. Unclench, unknot, unravel. Let go. ***Just relax.***

And if a tough situation arises, and it will, open and be present with that moment fully. Allow it to pass through and not imbed itself *in* you. Remember your body will remember! You ***will*** and ***can*** feel the moment of course, in its *full* experience, but let that life moment move ***through*** you, open to the need to resist, ***resistance will close you, just do not resist. And you will remain open.***

It goes without saying, that you will come up against circumstances and situations which will test, what feels like every fibre of your being. This is the spiritual path. **This is it!** *Life in motion, the spiritual practice of the highest order has begun, class is in session.*

The ever-evolving openness, non-resistance, acceptance, surrender and yes, forgiveness.

There will be no doubt times, absolutely, one hundred percent where you will feel you have failed, where closing off will feel safer than staying open, where resistance feels like bravery, where acceptance feels like you have been beaten, where surrender feels like weakness and forgiving the unconscionable, in-comprehendible.

There will be times you will feel you cannot go on, or let go, or forgive. You will flounder. Do not come down hard on yourself. There is no set date in which your assignment must be handed in. This is the work of a lifetime, and this is a lifetime of work. Loving work.

The difficulty is in its simplicity. But it is a continual lifetime, of evolving practice.

It takes loving conscious awareness to become open, and more importantly remain open.

It takes loving conscious awareness to remain present, it takes loving conscious awareness to come back to a state of wholeness and to continually remind yourself, *you can always do something to heal the next layer.*

It takes loving conscious awareness to keep coming back to the beginning to start again, and again………. and …. Again.

The Very Underestimated Hummmmmmmmm.......

Breaking the cycle of stress, anxiety, depression, of trauma, and even bad habits, is the key to freedom. It is something we can all do. You can, with awareness and a willingness to take daily action, and an openness to yourself, come to an **unwavering dedication** to break the cycle of your old self - 'when life comes along, you get knocked off your feet, mortally, and emotionally wounded.'

One thing you can do for yourself from this moment forward is to reach for one of the easiest tools you can use to incorporate into your day.

You can learn to feel more at ease in your body in the simplest of ways. To stimulate the vagus nerve which neuro science now agrees and explains, to calm your nervous system, and your mind.

The ventral vagal nerve, the twelfth cranial nerve is stimulated when you hum, causing the whole nervous system to relax. The whole body gets involved, and receives the chemical change, to relax and calm the body and mind.

So yes, *you can settle your whole nervous system, the whole body by humming. "Yes humming!"*

Science is now catching up to what the ancients, yogis, and sages, have known and been practicing for thousands of years. The OM is the sound of the universe, when you chant 'OM,' it helps to restore the nervous system.

It calms the mind and body. The ancient spiritual leaders, practitioners and lay people have been chanting and humming for thousands of years. Science can now prove what 'they' have known all along, and when modern medicine and the approach of the long-term talking therapies open their minds, look outside the box, then the mental and emotional health system will start to serve the individual in an all-encompassing approach.

We *cannot* segment or separate the body-mind connection. It is one, and it is my hope, that one day medicine will recognise this.

Humming to your favourite song can calm the body and mind enough for you to unclench, and start to soften, and over time open the blockages within you.

The mind will feel undisturbed, the dialogue not so loud, the restrictive walls you have built can come down. You are not in darkness like you may feel, the wall you have built like a master builder is preventing the light coming into you. *You* are preventing the light from reaching you.

Humming or chanting if you are so inclined and willing, opens you to a rhythm of relaxation, of calmness, and even tranquillity. Allowing little slithers of light to warm you, and invite you to remove one stone in the wall at a time.

You can feel more at ease in a very short time, when you hum.

The Bhramari Pranayama

The Humming Bee Breath

This is a powerful practice to calm the nervous system. Try it out!!!

There are many versions of this popular Pranayama, (breathwork practice), so please do not reject any other you may come across in the future.

Sit comfortably and settle into your breath.

Take a couple of mindful long inhales and long sighing exhales.

- Keeping the mouth closed but the jaw slightly parted. Exhale making it prolonged.
- Lift your elbows to shoulder level and close your ears by pressing in the tragus with your thumbs.
- Place your index fingers above each eyebrow, your gaze gently focused in between your eyebrows, close your eyes, and cover them each with the remaining fingers. Gently covering, not pressing into your eyes. Inhale.
- Breathe out through your nose making a humming sound.
- 'Mmmmmmmmmm' sound until you exhaled.
- Listen in a relaxed manner to the sound.
- Make sure the exhalation is smoothly controlled so the sound is uniform, even right to the very end.

- End the exhalation cleanly and do not turn it into a quavering over-lengthy sound marathon.
- Continue slowly, inhaling and exhaling until you want to stop.
- Inhale again through the nose, then exhale the Mmmmmmm.
- Try to sustain the Hummmmmm.

Repeat five to ten times.

This reduces blood pressure, reduces muscle tension in the face and temples. It can relieve migraines, is an emotional release and a good anti-stress exercise, improves concentration, relieves hypertension, calms the mind, and introduces one to deep meditation.

Showing Up

You can choose to break the cycle of stress, to not live in a nervous system reactive state, fight, or flight, or that damaging low grade level of a knotted stomach. *But it takes work and you must be willing to do the work, and this work is life-long.*

In no time you will start walking taller, others will feel your open heartedness, you will start showing up as the more healed version of yourself every day. The more you show up to yourself and others as a better version of you, you will start to heal deeply.

Cycles of negative patterns will be broken; you will show up to the world differently, others will *feel it*. *You* will feel it, and the world *will* respond.

First with your children, then your spouse, your family, your work colleagues, your town, and it will ripple out.

Eventually others will join your light, and it will ripple out from them, not only out into their immediate world, but so beautifully out of reach, healing one person at a time. Calming one person at a time, soothing one person at a time. This is what the world needs. Individuals, free from disturbance. Minds quiet and hearts open.

So, start humming the profound 'OM,' or at least your favourite tune, and you will start re-organising the body and mind in such a way, relaxation will become a part of your day. No matter what you are presented with, and if not in *that exact* moment, you *will* come back to the 'earthly home,' of your body and mind, ready now, to accept relaxation.

So, when life comes along, you can step up and respond to life in a more settled way.

The settled nervous system will become a new way of being, yet funnily enough, your natural way of being.

"Instead of seeing the rug
pulled from under us,
we can learn to dance
on a shifting carpet."

Thomas F. Crum

Hum,
sing out loud,
move your feet,
dance and belt out a song!
Quieten back down
and hum once again

Why Bother?

When you start breaking the cycle of being the old you, when you start re-building yourself from the ground up, you begin to feel more harmonious throughout your days, you are befriending your body, and learning to master your mind, so it is working for you on a more regular basis, *rather than you working for it.*

Your decision-making fires on all cylinders. When you make a snap decision, it feels right. You are living 'in-sync' more and more.

You feel at ease, in flow, and the world and universe are responding by expanding everything you focus on in a beautiful way.

But …… what happens when you are doing the work but those around you are not?

What happens when you must continually be in an environment where the other is not willing to look at themselves, and break the cycle of old stories for themselves?

What happens if you feel as though you are the only one who is growing? How do you handle those moments, that environment, if it is your spouse, boss, or family?

What happens when you feel as though you are breaking the cycles that no longer serve you but your spouse is not?

What is the point when it feels like it just all gets undone?

What if your spouse or friend is not willing to be open enough to even look? Or inquire?

You show up as the person you are becoming.

You show up as the more harmonious grounded person.

You show up as the better version of you.

You show up as the more healed version of yourself.

You show up as the lighter heart.

You show up as the more open heart.

You show up as a relaxed heart.

It can be a difficult situation when you must go back into an environment where others have not, or are not willing to do the work, or any work for that matter.

It can lead to the feelings of "why am I even bothering?"

"Why am I even trying to change my old story and break my cycle?"

It is frustrating, and can leave you feeling as though you are batting your head against a brick wall.

This is where the growth lies.

You either come to the realisation this environment is not for you, and yes this can happen, where you have outgrown another. You may then, consciously choose to remove yourself, so you can continue to move forward.

Or

You keep showing up as your more balanced, healed self, daily; knowing you are growing exponentially every time you show up...........to yourself; for yourself; and as yourself.

Rock Bottom

I want you to go belly up,
I want you to miss the boat,
I want you to run aground,
I want you to fall flat on your face,
I want you to come unstuck,
I want you to fail spectacularly,
I want you to hit rock bottom.

I pray that when you think you have hit rock bottom, the floor falls out from beneath you, that you fall so deep, it feels like you could emerge through to what feels like a foreign galaxy.

So far removed from what you think you know.

Where you have no choice but to search and emerge.

I pray that you are jolted awake, uncomfortably awake, so that you can awaken fully, and somehow in the same breath, it feels like slow motion, waking slowly with new sight, and a razor-like vision.

I pray that your discomfort is experienced so often that it becomes as comfortable as those unseen to the public, but fully appreciated 'elastic-less' thread bare PJs.

I pray that your screams become the silent of whispers, and your whispers become hair 'raisingly' deafening.

I pray you hit rock bottom, so when you have fallen as far as you can go, you finally realise the only way is up, and out.

That you come to know in that moment there is nothing left but possibility.

Where, as you have hit bottom, the ego, all falseness, and old stories have fallen away and stripped you bare, on the way down.

What a gift, to fall and fall, and hit, rock bottom.

To be left with nothing but infinite possibility.

I pray that you are so openly raw in this moment, that there is nothing false or untrue left.

Just a stripping bare of all false identity to reveal a not negotiable inquiry, a different perspective, and a realisation that the only way *is up and out.* The only way out, is to rise. Reach skyward.

I pray that you allow the bottom, the lowest you find yourself to be, in hitting rock bottom, the universal springboard from which to feel your feet push off from, catapulting you back into the light.

I pray that your pain, while sitting amongst the rubble, you become willing to explore the deepest, darkest, unspoken depths of your being, while collapsed there at rock bottom.

To find the courage, and willingness to reach out with arms and heart say, "I am scared, but I am ready."

And as you rise to your feet, thank the teacher, the guide, the guardian angel, who sat with you there,

And even if it does not make sense, defies all logic, and does not seem possible, but, sets your heart on fire, then make it possible.

I pray that you reach and reach again, trust and trust again, open, and open again, for this is the only way.

Walk toward your True North, however, that looks to you.

I pray that your rock bottom becomes the greatest of gifts, greatest of opportunities, and the most precious of blessings.

Stand up. Rise to your feet, and walk yourself out into the light.

It shouldn't be out of the realm of comprehension
to become the shepherd,

could it not be possible that you are
capable to lead?

Aren't you curious to discover what
is true for you?

Instead, society is teaching us we are sheep,

following blindly, unquestionably,

as we are rounded up into a direction we would
not have *consciously* chosen.

You are a boss!
You are the sole investor,
the CEO,
and the visionary for
own your life,
So be courageous, learn
your true worth, and
invest in *yourself*.

There is NO Doubt, it is Work.....

But it is Worth it.

Are you willing to work intently, lovingly, and wholeheartedly, for the next few weeks, months, or years to make real change?

As life continues to come along in all ways, are you willing to not lie down and not give up, are you willing to step up, step forward, even when you feel like hiding away?

When you are 'triggered' by a situation, this is good. This is a great opportunity for growth. The only opportunity for growth.

You cannot move through life and expect not to be triggered. You cannot expect another to behave a certain way to preserve your feelings from being hurt. You cannot expect another to have the same view as you, so your emotions are spared.

We are seeing, sadly, far too much of this in the world right now, whereby others are feeling offended by another. We must learn to, if we are to build resilience, find freedom within our everyday, begin to look at things differently. Then the things we look at will change. If we must voice our opinion, *we must go from saying, "you offended me." To, "I found that offensive." Because at the end of the day, what offends one, will not offend another.*

As a society, we must learn to agree to disagree. To be able to communicate and debate in a healthy way, whether it be a friend, spouse, boss, parent, or child, conversing with respect of another's view point, and knowing when to be quiet shows emotional maturity, emotional intelligence and is a continual practice and reward, all in the same breath.

The more you show up to yourself and allow this work to evolve, the better listener you become, the way in which you communicate will be more enriching and that peace you yearn for, will remain inside of yourself. It will continue to be unwavering, even when the other almost certainly disagrees with you.

You can learn to enjoy the world, within this lifelong work, until the so-called work, becomes you. This builds resilience, your back bone, and your attitudinal muscle.

Resilience is crucial, emotional intelligence is necessary.

When you decide to immerse yourself in this work, the moment you are presented with a trigger from a traumatic experience, or even an annoyance, rather than it triggering a full visceral response within your body…………..

Firstly, if it does, you will be able to observe and settle yourself more quickly.

And

Secondly, you will see it as another learning experience, to be able to then forge ahead with new knowledge and perspective once again.

When you decide, because remember it is your choice, to step up, be bold, courageous, and curious, you will no longer live in a continual nervous system reaction, of stress, and anxiety.

It takes work, it takes effort, but it is worth it.

Because……………

On the other side of this work …………..

is your healing,

on the other side of this work …………..

is your happiness,

on the other side of this work …………..

is your transformation,

and during all this work …………..

is your life.

A Trilogy of Ponderings

When life comes along,
be bold,
be courageous,
be curious,
be magnificent,
become........
UNSTOPPABLE.

Life may *start* from a
matter of chance,
But your life *will* become a
matter of choice.
And experienced *through* a
matter of choice.

You might feel as though
your life is working,
but,
may I ask you…….
Are you at peace?

Rewards!

When we work, we are rewarded. When we work, we get paid.

Effectively, it is a reward.

You work more, you work harder, you get more results! You work smarter, the sky is the limit!

We can apply the same principle within the practice of peace.

What starts as the desire for peace, then the want for peace, to the need for peace, over time, peace becomes the goal.

When you embark on showing up to yourself and for yourself, you will begin to be 'rewarded' within the practice of peace.

The world will start re-enforcing your practice.

The less you live from your wounded self, the more you will live from your higher self.

The need for justification will begin to fall away and you will start to see every day as an opportunity.

So, when life comes along, choose to do things differently. Live from your higher self, your future healed self, which will end up serving your nervous system. You will no longer live in a state of woundedness, of victimhood, or from a heightened nervous system, in flight, fright or freeze.

Your emotional home will look very different. In fact, you may even move emotional address completely!

Transformation, and peace is the reward.

The End

If the end is swift,
I hope the shock jolts you awake,
if the demise is slow, even painful,
I hope you take a torch, a light
to enter the long dark abyss.
I ask you to sit in the bloody, devastating
ruinous scene of the end.
I ask you to sit with your desperateness, and lay your head
on the pillow of hopelessness.
I want to ask you to lay down alongside
your anguish.
Can you be, fully in the suffering and agony of your own
mind
and still feel your heartbeat?
As your heart beats, in your moment of "how do I go on?"
Can you feel it beat for you, thump thump, thump thump,
thump thump
What can you hear in the space in-between?
Can you hear its message?
Can you feel the echoes of the rhythm in your mind, in
your ears, in your very existence?
Can you feel the stripping bare naked, the nothing left to
lose moment,
the very candid, "is this it?"
And with that question, a gateway…...
Where no end, that *is* the end, would ever have a gateway,
This end is the beginning.
This end, like *so many* endings, is the beginning,
A beginning of becoming aware of not only nature's seasons,
but the seasons within you.

if we were to hold onto one season forever, what our world and life would come to
look like, without that change.
The beginning of allowing your awareness to wander through what each season has to offer, as no season can begin without the other coming to an end.
The realisation that in your bloodied and catastrophic moment,
it has become an enriching compost and nutrient,
for a new season of self.
And in what you come to realise in your emotional,
physical, mental, and spiritual wintery season,
is that spring comes next.
The beginning of beginnings,
the creator of all creations, emerging from
dark to light.
Spring is always on the horizon.
Awaiting its bloom.
With sun on your face,
and light in your heart,
the brutal ending is but a memory,
as you step into your glorious beginning,
as your life transforms,
knowing this too shall pass,
as *everything,* has a season.

Every season lives
within you,
but
not all at once…
are you willing to let
go,
so, the next can come
forth?

All That is Left is You

When life comes along,

nothing seems to feel more difficult than when
you are left feeling exposed.

Where you feel you have been stripped bare for
the world to see.

And even more challenging, for *you* to see.

But when there is nothing left to hide behind,

and all else has fallen away,

what a gift, a turning point, a moment of evolution.

Then with arms wide open, face raised to the
heavens, with a "Yes! Let's dance! Let's do this!"

All that is left, is you.

Real, honest, vulnerable, and human.

Let life not wear you down,

but sculpt you into a one of a kind, the rarest of
gems, as life continues to come along.

No Longer Interested

It is interesting as life comes along, and you now live it with awareness, whereby you have delved into what is uncomfortable, have you noticed you begin to enjoy and soak up the depths of conversations? The raw, holding of the gaze, ears wide open, heart-to-heart conversations?

Have you noticed you become less and less interested in 'surface' chat?

Having become more aware of living my days with awareness, over the years, even in what seem like the small moments, most importantly what appear to be small moments, I am no longer interested in polite, scoot along the surface, idle chat, even fictional conversation. With either those I hold dear or those whom I do not know well or at all, I just simply feel I no longer want to waste precious time with half-baked truths, or 'polite chit chat.'

I want to know your heart. I want to know what makes you tick. I want to know what you ache for, what pulls at your heart strings, what you dream.

I want to hold the hand of someone dear who is sitting in **their** fire, awaiting to rise out of the ashes, where they only see blame of another, can only feel judgement, can only ask, "Why me? Why is this happening?"

While I want to tell them all will be well, I also let them know as gently as I can, "What part did you play in all of this? Where, and how long did you lie to yourself? Why have you chosen to carry this burden for so long? Why did you pretend to not see the truth? You deserted yourself, when your soul needed you the most."

To sit in the fire is brutal, to willingly walk yourself in is harrowing, to sit with another in their fire is a devoted act of love. To sit and burn together, to transform. These are the conversations, of full soul truths which light me up, invite my heart to expand, don't they you?

To rise out of the ashes of denial, half-truths, lies, white lies, habits, trauma, drama addiction, drug addiction, social media addiction, or alcoholism, is the life changing moment.

When life comes along, we can either choose to walk through or sit in the fire, or life will do it for us. In one moment, when everything changes and everything feels on fire, we have no choice but to walk on through, to burn away the sediment. The impurities. To rise anew. Leaving the debris behind in ashes, to birth your soul, you.

These are the precious moments and conversations to share with another, to sit with another, and roast and burn away the awkwardness, the falsehoods, the misleading, all that is not real.

Hold the hand of another when life comes along and sit in the flames together. Rise awakened, knowing we may have to walk through the fire or sit in the flames many times in this life time.

Rise

When we rise from the ashes,

we no longer view the world from our 'traumered',
triggered, or wounded model.

We no longer deny our wounds, speak from
our wounds, or live from our wounds.

When we rise, we heal our personality just
enough to realise where we went astray,
where we lied to others and ourselves,

where the excuses began, what we created within,
to not live fully.

When we rise, it becomes clear, healing is an
ongoing process,
but in that one moment, we release the weight of the past.

When we rise, we transform, knowing the difficulty and
suffering that we have experienced,
was the catalyst for change and growth.

When we rise, we rise with back bone,
fortitude, and resilience.

When we rise, we welcome possibility,
and the unknown, with curiosity
and excited anticipation.

When we rise, we realise we cannot be strong without first
being vulnerable.

When we rise, we come to know, inevitably,
we will have to rise again
and again.

"Step into the fire of
self-discovery. This fire
will not burn you,
it will only
burn what you are not."

Mooji

Think You Do Not Have a Choice?

That is a Choice!

When I was given the gift of contracting a virus many years ago, originally, I surely did not see it as a gift.

I was very sick for more than 4 years, and while I did not see it as a gift at that moment, I did recognise in myself the pushing I had done in my life. This illness had, in a very direct way reminded me that I had not been listening to my body. That I had wanted to slow down, to start to explore slow living, to take the awareness of my yoga practice off the mat out into my daily life, to become consciously aware of my thought habits, eating habits, and life habits.

But no. I chose to ignore the subtle but very direct whispers and signs. So, the universe provided what I could not do for myself at that time. *It slowed me down, for me!*

The very real realisation that I could not walk myself from my backyard to my back door, a whole ten to fifteen meters without the need to sit down and rest before I could even make it to my door was shattering to me. When I could not even bare the weight of a bed sheet on my body as it was too heavy, the pain was crushing.

A breeze on my kidney area even on the hottest of summer days, the chill too much to tolerate, the pain excruciating. Hot water bottles were the only way I could often get through.

Where even it seemed, my eyelashes screamed and writhed in pain.

Where to be honest, suicide knocked at the door of my spirit and beckoned with an alluring relief.

But as I learned the language of my body, the asking's of my soul, and the obvious prompt from my spirit, I began to put myself back together.

I listened, I obeyed, I honoured, I acted upon, I changed my thoughts, and made friends with my body and began to master my mind.

A new world was opening up to me, my world.

My mantra went from "I think I can" to "I know I can," to "I can" to "I am."

I whispered it, I said it out loud. I slowly built the strength to not only walk to the end of our road, a whole two hundred meters from our home, but also walk back, as Brett so often needed to pick me up at the end of that road, as I physically did not have it in me to walk back home.

As I nurtured my body and mind back to health, nursed and accommodated my physical needs, I gradually came back to life with a promise to always listen to my body, and even thank what became new sensitivities, I now found myself living with.

Food sensitivities, perfume on others, cleaning products, scented candles, lotions, fragrances, chemically sensitive all round left my body in a debilitating pain. But I came to thank my body in letting me know when an environment was toxic, *even when claiming to be 'clean.'*

And come back I did, with a spring in my step and strong fitness level, loving work. The social life looked different, but I was back with an affectionate appreciation, and finishing some long-term study, I was on top of the world.

And then............

Life came along.............................

A little stiffness in my thumb, and wrist a couple of hours later, before I was due to drive home, to being unable to lift my arms for the steering wheel. I drove with my knees and hand on the lower part of the steering wheel; it was all I could manage. Not safe I know. My rational thinking squashed with the pain.

Within an hour I could barely walk. A hot bath I thought....... Made no impact. The pain extreme, affecting my breath, to breathe deeply was not possible. Shallow breathing was all I could manage. I could not tell what part of my body screamed more. It was a mish mash of barb and razor wire, a hot blow torch and a constricting snake enveloping me.

I just needed an answer, and as the onset of pain was so fast, it was the first time in my life that I felt scared. The fear swarmed around me, and constricted me inwardly, and while I wanted so desperately to run and hide, stick my head in the sand, I also needed an answer. A hospital visit, blood tests and pain relief administered, which did not even touch the sides.

A doctor's call a few days later, revealed a new infection of the same mosquito born virus. Another infection! Worse this time!

"I cannot do this shit again!" through sobs to Brett.

"Yes, you can, you did it before, you'll do it again, you can do it," he said.

"I can't! It bloody nearly took five years to get over the first time! I don't have that kind of fight in me!"

A few days to fathom what had transpired, and the realisation of where my body was, once again, while I didn't have any fight left in me, *I did have the acceptance and the willingness to sit in the fire....... once again.*

It was a new level of rock bottom, in that fiery pit of despair. Hopelessness, distress, beyond the state of shock, and a sense of faithlessness. *There I sat. Alone.*

As the burning away began, as my layers were stripped away, it slowly revealed a sense of contemplation, of reflection. It was revealed, that in my previous recovery, naturally driven, but in my ability to reach and strive, I had started pushing. And................ "Had I forgotten the torment, of the perceived sense of failure, the lessons?"

Obviously, and very clearly, I had. *The universe had once again given me an opportunity to meet with myself.*

Lesson forgotten? Then new class, same topic – class is in session!

Meet the Injured Party

The Victim

I thought I had received the lessons. I thought I had grown. I thought I had mastered letting go of the judgement, of pushing, of comparing, of the victim mentality. That is how I gained back my health the first time. Why the hell was I back here again?

Clearly, I had unfinished business.

I had been given another opportunity to come face to face with all my victim way of thinking, with all my victim selves, which I thought I had dealt with, released, and moved on from.

I put my head down and bum up. I worked with my heart, I sat with my heart, even though at times it was excruciatingly uncomfortable and wildly beautiful all at the same time. I sat with my longing, and utilising my inner compass, to stay my True North.

I was not given ill health as a punishment, the body breaking down was not the lesson. The lessons lay within the feelings I felt WHILE I was ill.

You see, what I came to realise, if you break a leg, it is not the lessons you seek in the broken bone in traction, the lessons and clues lie in what you feel *while* you are motionless with a broken bone in traction.

This is where you meet yourself, the victim self. We all have one.

The victim self is within all of us. We all have one. The victim has you judging, comparing, whining, blaming, and excusing.

I thought I had left that behind. But here I was deep down in 'victimville'.

When I sat in the fiery pit, and allowed all the falseness to fall away and sat uncomfortably but honestly with the truth, I realised I felt jealous. Jealous! I felt a failure, I felt a sense of hopelessness and betrayal.

I finally understood, through meditating, reading, listening, *feeling, and sensing*, these were the feelings I needed to focus on. This is where I met myself, fully.

I could no longer turn away, the fears and judgements, my victim self was still alive and well. Whilst I thought I had previously let that stuff go, clearly, I had not. *Here I was, this time willingly sitting in the centre of the fire. Fully. Without scrambling and fighting to stay away from the heat.*

The illness was not the issue. The issue was what the illness invoked in me. All these feelings robbed me, of *me*, on an energetic level. My source of power had been acutely and then chronically interrupted and unfinished.

When we have deteriorated that much, it is *our* job to find out what builds our power source, once again.

This is what I set out to do. I realised, in my first 'aha' moment, that I had never celebrated my accomplishments.

I achieved and moved on, achieved, and moved on, setting sites for the next quest.

But now I was wanting to come face to face with all the parts of myself that felt less than. That made me feel a failure, jealous, envious, small, and fearful. All the parts I had hidden from view, even from myself.

The more I focused on what made me feel powerful, in an organic, healthy, wholesome, and energetic way, the more I liked who I was not only meeting, metaphorically and physically speaking, *but who I was spending time with......... me.*

And over time the victim self-shrunk, and the warrior, my white knight, became steadier, stronger, and influenced my days in the most profound ways.

Just over two years from the second diagnoses I received, I was once again bike riding, running, climbing mountains, and **celebrating** the smallest of achievements and appreciating every step along the way.

I was healing. Each moment in which I chose to rest my awareness on where and when and with whom I felt strong, and where, when and with whom I felt weak, even in my own company, particularly in my own company, no matter how minuscule, *everyday became an intriguing turning point.*

In what I thought to be tough decisions, anything from the food I ate or did not eat, to what I drank or did not drink, to the movies I watched or chose not to watch, to the company I kept or eventually did not keep, ended up being surprisingly easier choices, **when I allowed my body to guide me.**

Alignment

When I aligned myself with the victim, I suffered. When I aligned myself with my ally, the warrior, the white knight, I felt stronger. But it was not until I met the victim-self head on, face to face, did I really understand *in my bones*, that my life appeared to be built upon a victim foundation, and within a victim structure. Unconsciously. But now consciously aware, *I could not unsee it.*

I vowed to never come back to this place, I vowed and really made a commitment to myself to go on a life's quest to discover what made me feel strong, heart strong, spirit strong, soul strong, powerfully built from the inside out *and* from the ground up.

Not rowdy power, not cocky power, but a quiet, peaceful, unwavering, underestimated power which no one else sees, but is felt within, which brings you close to spirit, and your creator, in every way.

It was never about the illness. While there is no cure, I do live symptom free, and feel stronger and more aligned than ever. Only a subtle but *very* evident reminder, every few years, just to ask me "Am I still listening? Am I still aligned with the intuitive warrior? With the white knight?"

It was always about those emotions of the victim having been inside me for a long time, right back to childhood probably, certainly teenage and into adulthood. Jealousy, failure, envy, blame. *It was the illness which magnified the victim so gloriously that I could no longer look away.*

Ill health was the vehicle in which delivered the opportunity.

Face to Face

When you finally choose to face the victim,
A wild desire to run and hide envelops you.
But,
you tentatively pull out a chair for each of you to sit,
and settle yourself, as the conversation and realisation lays
bare the uncomfortable truth.
You jostle, to find an uncomfortably comfortable position
to face the least welcomed, but needed, truth you could
ever imagine.
Whereby the truth now reveals the victim as the trojan
horse.
Where maybe, for the entirety of your life, there has been
this cunning invasion, many times.
But now, an ally enters the gates of your being,
strong, elegant, courageous, a marvel to behold, as you feel
beyond the five senses,
and see clearly with no physical eyes, hear with no physical
ears and sense with no physical body.
There is no doubt the white knight, the warrior, has entered
the holy gates of the mind, and the true essence of you.
Drink it in, breathe it in and let the victim feel the breath
of the white knight,
of a warrior, in its face.
Feel the power build, preparing for the spiritual task at
hand,
a battle, which is often life long, sometimes until our death,
but now in this moment, comes to a head.
You surrender into the wisdom of the warrior, in what is the
continual brilliant advance, over the bloodied and battle-
weary victim.

As you fascinatingly focus on the white knight, the victim retreats with tail between its legs.

You know it will inevitably one day try again, knowing the victim breeds like rabbits,

it will be back tenfold.

However, you will be ready, as you have now felt the capability and power

of freedom.

From here on, you will only see gifts in having come face to face in this meeting with the victim self.

As you take the road of the warrior, you remain focused, like the white knight.

Aware of any ambush that may await you.

You are vigilant. And remain so.

And as your vigilance pans not only the horizon, but the deepest chasms of yourself while

following the example of the warrior,

a part of you still feels the predicted ambush imminent.

Then, there it is ……….. it is instant. Yet there is no stand-off, no battle this time, as the victim is out- numbered, out-weighed, out of its league.

It slinks away,

knowing now to watch from afar, knowing it has had its day with you.

It has grown so weak, a further battle would be useless, pointless and in vain.

For at one time, you blindly followed the victim, you now, eyes wide open,

follow the cues of the white knight, the warrior, feeling into what it is to walk in their shoes,

Until you became them.

The following eight pages are a few wonderings and wanderings of the mind

Times where I have often found myself sitting with a curious but quiet mind. A mind which I have simply let wander into a timeless world, the daydream, the meditation, the quiet sitting. A time whereby the pen finds its own wording, and shows me a different way of thinking, of being.

As I ponder................

The Musings of Sweet Nothingness

The sun weeps
And the rain draws up to the clouds
The rocks are light as a feather
And pebbles unmoveable
What comes down must go up
The moon shines the days
And the sun lights the night
Every thought a neon sign
Every spoken word falls silent
I sleep awakened
And my wide-awake days, asleep.
I am born old and die young,
The yellow brick road leads nowhere
And the rabbit hole…………. to enlightenment.
The mountains too deep to navigate
And the valley too steep to climb.
With closed eyes everything is revealed, eyes open………….
I feel blind.
It does not always make sense, this life………….
But when the call goes out, it is answered.
With the pact sworn, and the oath taken,
When life comes along, it is all go,
amongst the stillness.

What is the Hustle Without the Bustle?

It is the hustle and bustle of life,
But what is the bustle without the hustle?
We can hustle without the bustle,
But can we bustle without the hustle?

When I sit for a few moments,
Hustle and bustle free,
the contemplation of something we so often live in,
becomes evident in the pause from the
hustle and bustle,
in which I contemplate.
How ironic.

Wonderings

I wonder how I got here,
And then...... abracadabra!
The sun enters my heart,
the veil thins, then lifts,
a red morning for the Shepherd's warning,
A clue, change is on the horizon.
I look in awe at the colours, mesmerised by the haunting
beauty.
Change is coming.
Do I brace or do I open?
Do I do both?
It is not spiritually pretty, as I am brought to my knees.
As I remember the colours of the Shepherd's warning.
I remember I prayed for this moment at some point in
time, I prayed for this.
This rumble, this storm, this evolution within.
Where the evolution feels more like a revolution.
Great discomfort, excitement, tentativeness,
and knowing in my bones there is an imminent death
awaiting,
where I am asked to lay bare
to forge ahead and surrender, and surrender, only then to
forge ahead,
to question and accept,
as I lean into the seasons, I know this too shall pass.
It is rough, there is turmoil,
it is powerful and beautiful in its tenderness,
in its invitations, and in its force.
In the slap up the back of the head and the tender embrace
I weep.

I expel …… everything…... that is not mine, to fall away,
to burn up……
As my spirit anticipates, my soul remembers, everything
that was,
before I was here …….. and everything that will be, after I
am gone.

The Invisible Wrestle

It is the knee in the back, unable to fully breathe,
It is the sudden flip of a toss, beneath the bed sheets,
The head lock which denies a peaceful mind on your pillow.
The anxiety filled gut in the "do I, don't I?"
As the mind flips back and forth, the body follows and
tosses in sleeplessness.
It is the invisible wrestle.
It is the shallowest of breathing, somewhere, I am grappling
for a long in-breath and huge sigh,
Hoping to find resolution.

The sleepless night of indecision.
As you reluctantly but *willingly* step into the ring and
inevitably begin the unnecessary wrestle with 'the decision.'
A choice?................. is there one? Yes.
The choice? Is to *not* wrestle, but rather lean into the body,
lean your ear into its language,
into its knowing and allow *it* to be your guide.
"No" .... body clenches, tightens
"Yes" ....body opens........... or ....
Is it "No" .... body opens?
"Yes" .... body clenches, tightens?
Ahhhh...... the relief of the decision.
Outcome unknown .... that is okay.
Surrender and feel into *your why* moment, *the how* magically
appears in time, and always, *just in time.*

The wrestle of in-decision is a choice.
Lean in and feel with your ears,
listen with your body.

There is no need to enter the wrestling ring at all.
Know the language of your body, with no wrestling match
needed............. Decision made.

Body opens, peace of mind.
Simple as that.

The Company I Keep

Company has touched me in my loneliest moments,

I have felt the murmurings of forgiveness that were not my own,

I have felt grace enter me after the storm of rage,

Peace has rested her hand on a shoulder in my jealousy,

I felt God rub my back while hurling my guts up into a loo,

Sit with me on a bathroom floor while racked and ruined.

I have felt the guidance when it was too dark to see,

The door has closed with a slam! Or a gentle turn of the handle with a "that is not for you."

The divine has lovingly kicked me up the butt when I have needed it most,

And my angel has gifted me the energetic exchange of the stern look of a concerned parent.

My guides have listened intently with a nod of the head without the passing of judgement.

I have flailed, been lost, only to find direction,

I have been, ever so briefly………….. to different realms,

I have sat within, 'out of this world structures,' that my inner world immediately recognised,

And been given clear messages from the other side.

I have seen the faces of those from centuries ago, and those of who, I can only describe as a memory from the future.

I have been guided by the invisible,

And shaken awake by the stillness.

It is a paradox, this life, of beautiful opposites and hair-raising similarities.

The shattering, only to put yourself back together.

A novel in just one chapter, a thesis in just one word.

With no coincidences, just synchronicities,

a theatrical play, if written by another, would appear absurd......... too dramatic.

And yet.......... here we are.............

A carefully woven silk, soon to be cut into stressful pieces, into traumatic shapes, strips of loss, triangles of life's pressures,

Then with a heavenly golden thread, methodically chosen to create something stunning, a one of a kind.

Put back together.

The patchwork of a lifetime.

A coming together of the physical experience, heartfelt meetings, and unexplainable contacts.

A melding together of the explosive, the dramatic, the enlightening.

The grounding moment of birth and the climax of death?

Who knows.................

But the anticipation of what might be next, pulls me into this now moment.

Because that is all there is.

Dedicated to Jem, and The Woman of the Cypress Trees
(you know who you are)

Where we have established boundaries,
they become fortresses,
when the crumbling begins
as a little pebble, a speck of mortar,
hardly perceptible, until ....
the gigantic slabs of stone fall into
their own foundation.
The wanting to lay amongst
the rubble and create rubble angels
in the debris,
as you lay in the dust of what is to become your
new foundation,
the inquiring, and *already* known wisdom meet,
come together; an introduction from each other
in what can only be felt in *this* moment as ......
The beginning, the middle, and the end.

Symbolic Familiarity

Is it not the craziest moment when the next world is laid
out in front of you,
when a dimension so far away, is so familiar.
Where worlds run parallel to ours and occasionally, we get
a peek.
Where you see them and cannot help but stare, with a sense
of disbelief,
and in the same time, it is all that exists.
A timeline you have never experienced, but as unfamiliar
as it is,
unquestionably it exists, just as I breathe here now.
We are only beginning to unfold the natural, ancient, and
futuristic knowingness,
which appears to be as natural as sleeping, eating, and
breathing.
The language and silence of these worlds fully understood,
an ancient language in symbols,
mind-blowingly intricate beyond human understanding,
yet nothing has felt more intimately recognisable,
never more known.

The Impact – *You* Decide

Magnetic North

The pull is tempting, it draws you out, and often looks shiny, new, it sparkles.

It waves its northerly arms in the 'come hither' motion, "This way!"

Others are going, "I should too,"

Like minded company in droves, it feels comfortable, it feels good, "it must be right, so many others are going."

But just when I almost 'get there,' 'there' moves, pivots, swivels. So, I do too.

Where to go?

I follow the north bound crowd, only to feel swept along, following the tracks, never having been there, other's foot prints I tread in, right in front of me, the designated North Track.

The company of the masses no longer quench my thirst for knowledge.

I am parched, even though others appear to be quenched,

I am starved, although the abundant surface seems flush.

I am almost there, then .... 'there' moves once more.

But achievements, collections, experiences, conversations, signalling an end point in which we search, relationships are born and embellished along the way, but are they healthy? And yet again, we move.

Another shiny object competes for our attention, and like a school of fish we change direction,

and continue............. moving, doing busy, but not getting anywhere, busily doing, it looks like achieving, but not accomplishing anything, no fulfilment, no contentment.

We are constantly doing, but missing the subtle, and very, obvious.

Always seeking but never finding. Exploring stillness, but never still.

Always yearning and never fulfilled.

True North

The pull is direct, no shortcuts, but *very* direct.

I may pivot, but the pull is constant, my internal compass aligns, and stays aligned, never wavering.

As doubt creeps in, "have no doubt," speaks into my ears, and lands in my heart.

The shiny, the crowds, the noise dissipate, but …………

Glossy sign posts ahead,

"This way!"
"Turn left."
"Go back!"
"Detour."
"Turn right."
"Speed limit change."
"On sale!"
"Buy now, Pay later."
"We will teach you what to think!"
"10% down, take home now!"
"New Addition."
"Latest release!"
"Limited time!"
And yet …………………

The internal compass does not move. Does not waver. No blinkers needed, I simply pass by without any attachment or want, or fear of missing out, or being alone.

No need to re-calibrate, it is pulled to me, keeping me aligned with True-North.

Alone, but not lonely.

Listening, observing, feeling unsure? Sure.......... Then the resolve.

The hushed, noiseless but definite, bigger than you, YES!

No foot prints ahead, just yours in the moment, and what you are leaving behind, **and** your invisible, but palpable guidance.

No shallow chit chat of blah, blah, blah.

Only clear, concise hearing and listening, from the non-highlighted sign posts,

Just the True North pull, a silent calling, which calls everybody, but very few listen.

The personal and internal sign posts, of simply *feeling* for 'the way.'

For this is the way. The way to True North. It is not popular; it will not be crowded. It is a lone road for your feet only. And as you trek, and navigate, you will find the odd True North trekker, not by what they wear, or the lingo they speak, but by their True North compass which beams authenticity, a quiet air, a no "look at me" presence.

Just a real discoverer refusing to follow the masses and speak the latest trendy talk, but a beacon for others. And while you may go

in what seems like the opposite direction, to your fellow 'True Norther,' you always spot and feel the authentic one.

The unexplainable inspiration ignites from within, always guiding, always the compass, for you to seek your True North.

When life comes along,
Would you dare look?
Will you dare listen?
Could you dare speak?
Would you dare dig?

So, you can learn to see
So, you can open your senses to hear, to listen,
So, you can live the truth you speak,
So, you can finally uncover, the cover-up.

The 'Date'

I love allowing the words to spill out across the page,

I love the knowing in that sometimes I have no idea where it will lead,

I love the haste in which often my hand simply does not move fast enough, or seems to even keep up with the words in my head.

I have even come to love the sporadic entries, knowing that when they come, there is something worth sharing.

I have learned to love the 'writer's block,' where I have come to know this is my pause.......... Creations brewing. It is here I have also come to know, creation must be expressed differently, during this time.

Gardening, food, dress, painting. Until it is ready for the season of spring, for words.

Then, the droplet of a word, suspended in space, momentarily entertains a thought, the thought, a beginning of a new relationship with that word, and its meaning, and as we start to 'date,' a sentence is formed. I sit with a cuppa, allowing them to entertain me, and I entertain the random word which progressively builds, into paragraphs, then blossoms into chapters.

And as I go from 'dating' a word, I savour a possible sentence, as it constructs its own build, realising this could work, a full-blown relationship, now serious, is taken to the next level, and a journal takes shape, a book birthed, even if just for my eyes to only ever read.

The dating is the exciting part, as I spend time with words like adventure, abundance, addiction, attraction, then tentatively touch on trauma, thrilling, 'the turnaround,' and transformation. As I spend time with support, surrender, simplicity, seeker, spirituality, it leads me back to commitment, connection, creation, communication, centred, then whimsically winds me through to wonderment, wonderful, why, wisdom, willingness, and funnily enough folds itself back on flow, freedom, fruitful, forget, flexible, focus, flourishing, opening itself to, 'Om,' then to the simple "Oh" and onto once again seductive and service. Off to Vikings………...

Not sure where that came from, but stay with me, which leads me to vitality, vibrant, visionary, then to a no holds barred holistic, hard, hurtful, humour, health, harmonious and honest.

A moment of a word seemingly from left field, like trailer-top, leads me to trailer-park, to top of the mountain, leading me to words like stumbling, sedentary, and then to sanguine and eventually through to symbolism and subliminal.

As this relationship deepens, simple words form curious pictures in my mind, then build a mini story. It is the fascination of how just one word that my mind lovingly seems to fixate on, winds itself in and out in my sleep, in my wakefulness, sequencing a delicate sometimes bold tapestry of communication, even if just for me.

I am not an academic, at all, but I love words, I love writing. I sometimes wonder what my English teachers would have thought, now knowing where my meanderings ended up. I wonder, but I do not care, as I simply just love to write.

The organics of layering word, sentence, paragraph, chapter, journal, and book.

I look and feel in awe, wonderment, and disbelief in a true believing way, that with it all, it comes back to a seed of a thought, of just one little, but mind-bending, mind-blowing word.

It is the start of it all.

Then we start to date.

5 Days, 4 Nights
A Sabbatical

The following nine pages are musings, coming through from meditations, insights and simply being still. Straight out of my journal, *just as I wrote it.*

For my 50th birthday, I took myself out into the middle of the Australian scrub, on a beautiful property, with not another soul around. A day for every decade. Just me, myself, and I.

Basic food, camp kitchen, a swag, a tent to retreat in, for the rough weather which was forecast, my journal, and I was set.

Wednesday Entry

A day to honour each decade. Fifty! Where did it go?

A celebration, celebrated in September, November? Fire ban. I wanted a fire. I knew this to be a big part of the five days. Fire, for me was to be a part of the ceremonies, the rituals, the prayers, the honouring's, the 'letting go's.' So here I am. Alone.

1st day. Setting up camp, sorting food, bedding, *"yes,"* I brought extra padding! Did I mention alone? Has not sunk in yet. Gather wood, get fire going.

Bed, done. Bush kitchen, done.

Early dinner, easy avocado and roasted sweet potatoes. Wash up, stoke fire.

Alone. Alone. Alone. Alone .... alone. Shit.

As my brain circles back on clients I did not call back, bills that I didn't get to and are due tomorrow, my mind is still well and truly on home. I sit.

I get up, I sit, I get up, I sit. "Did I forget my blanket? No. phew." Sit down again.

I let out the first of what was to become many sighs. Was I even breathing?

I am now. Consciously breathing.

Walk up to the hill where the mares are. Only to find a dozen kangaroos, and two boxing. They do not see me at first, so am able to witness this gorgeous display of nature at dusk.

The girls (the horses-mares) do not see me, but I am content with the sun going down and the colours painted across the early evening sky. "I am really on my own! For 5 days! Holy shit!"

I sit at the fire and stare, and listen to the unfamiliar yet completely natural sounds of nature, different to the sounds during the day.

A little nervous, restless, what to do................ "Should I meditate? A cup of tea? A night walk? No."

I go to bed, a little nervous and try and settle down in my swag. I am warm and thrilled I can see the stars while laying my head on the pillow. I close the zipper for the night, and fall into a restless, comfortable, uncomfortable, warm, awakened yet dreamed sleep.

Hips, legs, back hurt. Will need to do something about that.

Thursday Entry

Awake at 4.30am, unzip and wow, the morning……… the breeze, sky, and clouds start welcoming me into the day.

I hear the thud of roos, nearby, nervous, so dark, but they are only roos. I lay in and take in the sky, but soon need to move. Hips, knees, low back. Sore.

Some coconut water, fill up my hot water bottle, on the back, ahhhh……….. Grab yoga mat, and off to the hill to greet the day with a yoga practice. The practice feels agitated, clumsy, and not in tune. And yet, feel grateful that I practiced.

Hot lemon and water, forgot herbal tea! Stoke the fire. Rice porridge, and flick through my journal. Then……… I realise I am alone. Alone. I do not need to rush, go anywhere, do anything, be anything to **anyone**. Just here in the bush, with the morning calls, dewy scents, and aromas.

As I just sit, a kangaroo not 20 feet away jumps through my camp. Stops, in surprise and as I bid him "good morning," his ears forward, alert, but not scared, we share a moment.

He hops a couple of paces and stops again, looks at me, and again, and again. He took his time, and on he went.

Back pack on, yoga mat, and myofascial balls, water and off I go. Walking, walking. Greet the mares, and continue to walk.

I am asked to sit on a rock, it is meditation rock. I didn't just want to sit; I was *asked* to sit. I have heard of the 'others,' natural structures, rocks, trees, streams, and of course creatures., where a conversation can take place as evident as if someone is with you.

"Come sit. I am here for you tonight, it is tonight."

"I am not ready. It is cold, no shelter."

"Go and prepare. Tonight, we share together."

Something takes place.

I roll out the yoga mat, balls, and spend the couple of hours having a myofascial release and craniosacral session. A cool breeze, but warmth in the sun. I take off my track pants down to my knickers, my white skin soaks in the spring sun.

My body feels new and more relaxed, open to receive. I pick some gum flowers, wattle and together with the rosemary sprigs I brought from home, I started the 1st ceremony.

Warming some water on the fire, I stripped down naked. Stood in the sun and dappled shade, had a warm outback shower around the fire and so began my 1st coming back to soul ceremony. The shower was intuitive, and I conversed out loud to God, Jesus, Buddha, Mother Earth, Father Sky, the others, and all sentient beings, spirits and souls of past, present and future.

I was being welcomed back into a community so often forgotten, or removed a little, due to daily life. With jewellery that is special to me, wedding band, engagement ring, ring and bracelet Joshua made me, 2 rings, tree of life and diamante rings Hunter gave me, Hopono hopono bracelet, tigers eye ring, and bracelet.

Sandalwood, cedarwood, and wild orange with coconut oil is massaged into my whole body, as I prepare for a wedding ceremony, the second in my life. The first to the love of my life, and now to the life and love of all that is.

The lace flow-'iness' of the pink and cream long delicate dress, slip over my body. The knitted long flowy coat falls and drops naturally over the dress. I gather my posy of wild flowers and rosemary, a piece of Palo Santo wood I brought from home, light it, and allow the aroma filled smoke to smudge me, the flowers, and the fire.

And so, the marriage ceremony to soul, to self, to earth, to sky, to the creator of all that is, began.

My words are private, for me and for all that is, between only us. I may even forget the exact words in years to come, but the vibration of this ceremony will be forever etched in my mind, will flow in my veins, and be part of my soul.

Grace was present in that ceremony, God was the witness, the creator of all that is, a divine presence I cannot do justice to, or even begin to explain, was with me in amongst the gum trees. God allowed grace to step forward and I allowed grace to enter every part of me.

As I stood by the fire, the smoke followed me, it hadn't for the entire ceremony, but now it followed me. As my long dress cascaded and fell behind me, I kept gently walking to miss the smoke, stand still, move again, stand still, move again.

The message was loud and clear, "Just as you move and dance with the smoke, to miss it, move again, as it follows you, move again, side step, step back, side step, move forward, side step, in keeping moving, you *can* remain still inside.

This fire is life. Life will come at me, duck, and weave, to and fro, zig and zag, this is life!

"As life comes at you, can you remain still inside?"

This was the speech which the creator of all things conveyed and shared.

Sitting in my flowing dress, it gently wrapped around me as I sat cross legged around the fire, eating a celebratory lunch, the uniting of and honouring of all the elements, earth, air, fire, and water. North, South, East, and West. God, Christianity, Christlike consciousness, Buddha, the native American Indian wisdom, the sages of yoga, the energetic work, flow, and openness of the chakras, *all* come forth and come in.

Hours later, as I rise from writing these words, I am astounded to see a group of gum trees, 2 large. I somehow didn't see them before, 1 male, 1 female. The female has her 'legs' parted as the male 'enters' her, and yet ....

Could it be me, arms open wide as I was around the fire as grace enters,

And ......

Right alongside those 2, is a single gum tree, with 7 bridesmaid gum trees. They have a vine, mistle- toe type vine hanging from them as if they are holding bouquets, and I am the centre. It's as if they are all honouring and paying tribute to my ceremony, and yet it was me paying tribute and honouring them.

Friday Entry

Meditation at the rock last night, ceremonial, chanting, using sticks, finding rhythm, my rhythm? The earths? That of the universe? All of ours collectively I feel. I felt good.

The chant will be with me for a long time. Prepared for an 'all-nighter,' a distinct message......... "Go to bed, this is enough for now."

Restless night, loads of pain, breathe through it.

Stoke the fire, hydrate, an apple to share with the girls, and yoga in their paddock, a little nook out of the wind. The grass, wispy, it calls, "lay on me." Great interest from the girls, "what is she doing?"

I face the sun and open.

My variant on Salute to the Sun for today.

ARMS UP

- I open myself to you, to all that is.
- I open to receiving.

FOLD FORWARD

- I surrender and let go of what I cannot change

LUNGE WITH A TWIST- ARM UP

- I am strong, I am open to my strength

DOWNWARD FACING DOG

- I ground in my breath
- I ground and sink into my knowing

LUNGE TWIST – ARM UP OTHER SIDE

- I am courageous
- I open to my full courage

DOWNWARD FACING DOG

- I centre in my breath
- I centre and sink into my inner knowing, past, present, and future

MOUNTAIN POSE – ARMS UP

- I open myself to the possibility of all that is impossible.

MEDITATION

On breath - restless
On chakras - restless
On sourcing - restless
On Bruma Diya Bindhu – (3rd eye) - whoosh! I am there…...

Thankfully the energies around sense me and honour my struggle. I focus, restless, refocus.

Even with sourcing, I am not deep. "I will have breakfast and come back after brekkie and with that"…………… A gust of wind so strong it pushes me back on my butt and in my centre.

"This is exactly why you need to stay. You are not done. In the depths, are where the treasures lie."

I smile inwardly, and restlessly settle again. I am encouraged to practice Brumhadiya Bindhu breath.

Sinking straight into Ajna chakra, whoosh inwardly, deep, and there I stay.

When I edge out, and come back, I go to move and move my legs. The pain and pins and needles are intense, knees screaming and yet …………. Feel 'a welcome home.'

Friday Afternoon Entry

The camp is re-arranged as best as I can, as I wait for the weather to change. I have packed everything and cleared a space so to cook in tent, if necessary, tonight, and tomorrow.

Keep walking around in circles, is the tent water proof? Who knows? I will tomorrow morning!

I wait with a slight apprehension, have collected more wood and that which I have, has been bundled together in a compact pile so I can hopefully cover it to keep it dry.

I am as prepared as I can be, now to let go. My habits show up in this preparation. I keep looking at the clouds as if to will them away. Ask them to be gentle.

But life is not gentle, so why should a Friday night camping out for my sabbatical, and in some ways a vision quest, be any different? I am prepared, so now let go. I will face the rest when it happens. And……... I will handle it. What is the worst that can happen? ………… I will get wet, the tent rips from the strong winds, gums trees come down, or at least, decent size branches.

With everything packed away, I sit on the ground and write in preparation for the death circle, shadow work. The stuff I don't or ever want to look at. I *do* ………... but I *don't want* to.

I will prepare myself shortly and enter the circle, only leaving when it feels done.

Saturday Entry

Restless night, no sleep, a lot of pain in legs, feet, back and hips. However, was able to keep treating as best I can with little room in the swag. Thank God for my new sleeping bag. If it hadn't been for that, I would be very wet. Heavy rain, swag soaked, but .... I am quite content, the closing in is what was challenging at times.

Initially, the swag felt claustrophobic, but I was able to watch the stars on the 1st couple of nights. Last night, batten down the hatches. Breakfast in the tent this morning. Still raining. Clouds start to part.

And I prepare my circle, the circle of death, letting go.

Morning meditation as the sun comes up.

2 gum trees, brilliant pattern from shedding their bark call to me.

The twin hearts!

It is "no," to being the circle of death, it is to be the circle of shedding. I plan to write on paper and release but the twin hearts have other ideas. They offer up their bark, a few strips, so shapely, to take home? Beautiful. A gift from these two hearts.

"Write on these, burn them, offer them up to the fire and release them."

I feel the community of trees (gums) that live here, breeze in their agreement.

I am ready, pen in hand, I take a piece of bark. I don't know where to start ………….. so, I just start.

Before long, a spewing of rage, fear, jealousy, resentment comes flooding in.

The loss of the last 50 years, yes, this sabbatical is for my 50th. Tears come, my voice loud, intense, scared, angry, regretful, I question, I ask, I plead. I write.

On the bark from the twin hearts, as I write, it all moves through me. One word at a time. One sentence at a time. One exclamation point at a time. One feeling at a time.

Whatever is taking place transmutes it all and I am just left with steadiness in breath, thought, heart and gut.

It is done.

I place the bark with my words from my shedding circle on the fire. I have shed all I needed to for this season. Yes, shedding, letting go, dying, so new energy, birthed ideas can come in, will always take place.

For me this time, it was the obvious judgement, the lies, the coverups, the bullying, the damn 'V,' it scares me. My fear feels incredibly different to many others. I felt alone, estranged, judged, vilified, and punished. The world in 2020, 2021, and possibly 2022. Other things, jealousy, envy, have now passed through, and **WE WILL** BE OKAY!

One surprised me ……. The ending of my periods, the honouring of them. The end of my child bearing years. I mourned the loss of them from a deep place of resonance.

All those years of pain, inconvenience, push throughs, the lack on my part of not honouring the wisdom that came through.

When I finally wised up, I did not have them long enough. And now .... menopause. Moving from one phase to another. The mourning was deep and yet the lessons of wisdom that are coming through and will no doubt continue to come through in my next glorious phase of life, will be nothing but heartfelt and beautiful.

No workshop could have provided me this content with self, with source, the creator, the divine, like these 5 days have.

And now that the fire has cleansed, released, and finalised the shedding, (for now.) The ceremony of gratitude and appreciation is to begin. As I prepare, the sun pokes through the clouds, the weather has assisted me fully in all rituals, ceremonies, and meditations. It has been a remarkable assistant, the answers have come in a gale force wind, if only for a moment, to die down for me to reflect, the wind has raged with me, enticing me to keep going, "Let it *all* out!"

The soft breeze gently settles my tears, the sun comes out as I contemplate or meditate. It has been quite the assistant for my first sabbatical. I know it will not always be like this.

I heat water on the fire, stripped down to how nature brought me into this world. I cannot tell you how it feels to be fully bare, naked, in the bush amongst the gum trees! A warm bathe to cleanse, and wash away the last of any debris from the shedding ceremony.

This outback bathing is also ceremonial. Essential oils, of Australian Sandalwood, Cedarwood and Wild Orange with light coconut oil to massage in afterwards. The breeze is cool, the sun soaks warmth back into my bones.

I say a prayer and give thanks to the committee of kangaroos, rosella's, blue wrens, maggies, galas, the echidna, and 6 gorgeous girls, (mares), gum trees who not only allowed me to share their space, along with the treasured and much loved owners of this land, but gave their blessing.

I walk the hill anti clockwise this time to finish my solo retreat. A walking meditation, slow, with intention. I thank each area for supporting me, whether it be for yoga, meditation, setting intention, prayer, myofascial release, craniosacral therapy or simply observing.

I hope to come back here one day but if not, I will, I tell each area, carry it in my heart and mind. This has been a transformational experience. One that will stay with me for a long time, and one I hope to share with others, which came through very powerfully during this time. Something I had not thought of really, or not seriously.

The depth I could sink to, and explore, the shadow self that haunted, the rise of my next life phase, the display of appreciation and gratitude could not have been experienced with less time.

5 days, 1 day for each decade I have been on this planet.

"Be The Hill"

Most search for the majestic, the spectacular, a mountain top which is solid, unmoveable and reaches for the heavens.

Some search for a creek, a brook, or a stream, there is a notion of flow and a motion of ease often pertaining to "go with the flow."

Few sit under, or by a tree, listening to its language via the rustling of the leaves. The foundational roots go deep, and wide, they steady the tree, allowing it to still bend 'to and fro,' in all the seasonal winds and breezes.

A rock or a bolder is grounded, unmoving, and has wisdom gathered through the ages. A handful will sit with 'rock.' One of the many of nature's wise, as all offer guidance, solace, and invite us to draw on the qualities they all represent to us, to you, and to me.

Only a few seek the hill. It is easily passed by, as it is not a mountainous marvel, and not necessarily spectacular, it may appear to pale in comparison, compared to that of a mountain. Hills are more common. Not everyone has their breath taken away with either the view, or the desire, to climb and conquer the peak.

It is not a stream, creek, or brook, it does not necessarily offer 'go with the flow.' It does not always speak in sound, like the rustling of leaves, either on its own or one of many in a forest. It may not have the character of a rock or bolder, no ....hills can be passed by, walked over with little needing, or wanting to know its language. Yet here I walked, and am asked to sit, time and time again.

"I have what you seek, I know what you already know. I come in many different characters, wooded, treelined, grazed by cattle, heritage scrub, or baby green grass, and the high desert wonder. I blend in just enough that I am not covered by crowds of other humans.

I ask only a few to get to know me, which is how I like it. Only a few to converse in a silent language which is timeless, or out-loud; to be carried out to the ethers.

I may not have the magnificence of a mountain, but I still rise above the surrounding land, gifting you wondrous views. You can see me from many angles and can view the outlook, which changes often daily and certainly seasonally. I am sturdy, open, resilient, spacious, no two parts of me are ever the same. I rest in the knowing that a few will sit and spend time with me, absorbing my qualities.

I may not be spectacular, that would make me busy, with humans everywhere. No. I am not asking for foot traffic, I am asking for heart and soul awareness.

I am unique, all hills are unique just as you are dear human, who comes to sit and be with me."

This is a message which flowed through to me just before I packed up from my sabbatical.

Revenge

While you may feel lifeless inside, you are alive.

The world against you.

An atomic wasteland within, you will survive.

While you may feel embarrassed, or powerless, self-esteem and strength while feeling as though they are eluding you, still organically run through your veins,

You may think these things evaporated the day you were first violated, but they can never be taken from you, not ever.

You may feel your light has been diminished, snuffed out.

But it has not.

You can do this, you can do this for yourself, for your daughter, your son, brother, sister, parents, your friends, your community.

A violation, a trauma can either define you as a victim or as a warrior.

While you cannot be untouched by what happened, not at all.

You are, and have always been touched by an intrinsic and intuitive strength, courage, and spiritual prowess.

You are a powerful woman. Powerful human being.

The ultimate revenge is to succeed and win in life, but what does this mean?

To choose to be full of joy, 'joy-fullness,' happiness, fulfilment, contentment, and open to peace.

No one will save you,

But you *can* save yourself,

Your life raft is a heart open to life, open to lessons, curiosity, insights, once again joy, exploration, love and happiness.

You have got this; you can do this.

You want revenge? Be happy.
You want revenge? Be joyful.
You want revenge? Educate with love.
You want revenge? Get curious.

You want revenge? Spread the meaning of what it means to be courageous, strong, and open in healing.

You want revenge? Do not allow one crippling moment in time, (even if for years) to continue to be in your present moment.

You want revenge? Hone in on your skill set, mastering your mind, opening your heart, and let the life sparkle in your eyes once again.

This type of revenge is sweet, oh so sweet. It is sacred, and beautifully genius.

It is the gift that keeps on giving.

You grow, expand, deepen, and evolve in every conscious choice, and in every aspect of your life.

This is where you bow your head to your heart, inhale your wisdom and fling your arms wide open and say, "YES!"

Rest Your Head in Peace Tonight

When life comes along,
and all you want to do is hide,
to batten down the hatches
and assure safety from the rising tide.

You know what you do here matters,
and at the same time doesn't, challenging our belief.
Hiding will not solve a thing,
it is a temporary false sense of relief.

When you are terrified, frozen stiff and can't,
dig deep, move forward you must.
Otherwise, the past can stick to you like glue,
and life will leave you in the dust.

Stand tall, breathe deep, release,
that jargon that passes your lips won't impress,
for life will keep on coming, that's true, so be true.
Is it now or never? Is this the test?

Only you know, what inner language you speak,
what lays on the pillow with you at night,
for when life comes along, what matters is,
you have done your best to make it right.

Could you rest your head in peace tonight?
And practice your sense of ease,
because at the end of the day, it all matters
and nothing does,
so, allow your heart to beat in peace.

Sweet Revenge

You want revenge?
Have a killer smile, light up a room.

You want revenge?
No longer silence your understanding.

You want revenge?
Succeed.

You want revenge?
Decide to heal anyway.

You want revenge?
See your past as educational blessings.

If you think it was all taken from you,
Then by definition you have nothing left to lose.
You want to get sweet revenge?
Then you better get started on you.

Passion

There have been many times where you have been either told or heard, "Follow your passion!" those three words have ignited a multibillion-dollar industry. Some of our greatest artists have created and shared with the world from their place of passion. From movies, books, podcasts, art, and music, through to fireside chats with friends. It has possibly been the most common advice given and heard over the years, decades, and even contemplated for centuries.

If you are lucky enough to know what your passion is, that is invaluable. You can do what you love, love what you do, from your work, career, creativity, and hobbies, to your partner in life. You do great work, you can create, excel, and achieve, predominately with what feels like little effort.

Your passion can give you an edge in everything you begin, pursue, continue, and complete. When you are following your passion, you give a 110% week after week, month after month, year after year, for the most part, effortlessly. Because your passion becomes your fuel.

It is not always easy to find your passion, in fact, if you can't, don't, or haven't, it can cause a feeling of confusion, inadequacy, that finding your passion is for everyone else, and for you? Maybe not even attainable. But what if you have found a passion?

When I think about it, I have had different passions at different times in my life. I have never had one passion in which I have totally followed. I have had times where I have followed my passion for a very short time, until the next passion was discovered. Sometimes a passion has overlapped with another creating a multifaceted experience, simply through following 'a' passion, not just one.

If you don't have a passion or feel frustrated that you haven't found one, cool your jets. Simply get curious. Curiosity is incredibly valuable! Simply becoming curious, has allowed me to dabble and mess around over the years, and through dabbling, funnily enough passion has been discovered literally from first, being curious, then just allowing myself to play. Sometimes a new passion was not unearthed, but the realisation of just liking something, or loving something was stumbled upon, and sometimes I simply just had fun experiencing something new.

This is what is beautiful about venturing down a road of becoming curious and then to dabbling! Not everyone knows what their passion is. You maybe struggling to find one. But you know what? That is perfectly alright.

Curiosity is having a desire for adventure, or learning or exploring something new. Curiosity can be whimsical, light hearted, it can feel like an unexplainable need to inquire, to ask, to have a go, it can be surprisingly fearful, and at the same time exciting. Fearfully exciting and excitedly fearful! Who new!

You can become quite skilled in something you were once curious enough to dabble in, and over time, it may turn into a passion, it may not. But that is okay, look at what you have discovered along the way!

What have started as passions in my life, some have remained, some I have out grown, some I have moved on from, some have fallen away. Some gently and surprisingly came back into my life, only for me to feel more passionate than when they were first discovered.

Over the last 45 years, my 'passions' have included horse riding, coffee, spirituality, yoga, writing, hairdressing, poetry, gardening, travelling, playing the piano, teaching, cooking, politics, music, chocolate coated Brazil nuts, hiking, running, snow skiing, drawing, and sketching. Most of these are still passions today, and some are not.

When Passion is Not Enough

Maybe you are desperately trying hard to discover your passion for the first time, or your passion has grown wings and flown away, or turned to dust. No amount of 'follow your passion' will ever be enough when it is eluding you.

Your passion can sometimes take a back seat during different stages in your life. Chronic illness, grief, anxiousness, fear, doubt, depression, boredom, exhaustion, embarrassment, insecurity, or loneliness.

I have had times in my life when even the passion I felt for something had not been compelling enough or convincing enough to raise me up with enough enthusiasm to even start my day. It has even gone so far, whereby, I could not have given a damn about my passion in those moments. Not at all!

Where previously my passion had given me the necessary fuel to keep me going in times where things looked impossible, looked hopeless, not viable, downright difficult, or where doubt had threatened to derail a project. There were more than many moments in which passion simply did not suffice.

When chronic ill health robbed me of any clear, convincing, get up and go, and the most necessary of energy levels to even get off the couch, which kept me reclaiming that horizontal position time and time again, in pain, discomfort, hopelessness, where giving up seemed so effortlessly peaceful.

A peace in which I craved.

My passion did not save me in those moments, my passion did not lift me up, inspire me, fuel me, or raise my energy levels. It simply was not strong enough.

In these times there was only one thing that lifted my half dead body from the couch, dried my tears, and gave some reprieve from the insane full body pain, one thing that got me up and out, got me to continue. *One thing which surpassed even the most powerful of passions, and that was discipline.*

The discipline of many little practices over the years, some seemingly feeling insignificant at the time, obviously became ingrained in my body and well established in my mind. It was during these difficult times, that the realisation in being able to master my mind became priceless.

There have been times in my life, many times, where passion was not enough. It was discipline that dragged my sorry arse off the couch or out of bed. Got the ball rolling, that hauled my pained body into even the smallest of movement. A gentle short walk, restorative yoga, a benign stretch, which became the building blocks to once again be in the position of openness, physical strength, and mobility. Discipline in health, both mental and emotional, gave me the wherewithal to continue.

People underestimate discipline, but discipline gives us the direction to explore, start, continue, finish, *begin again*, and to stop.

Discipline gives us freedom.
In fact, discipline = freedom.

Discipline enabled me to do things that needed to be done. To do the things that seemed physically impossible, that were not fun, and aren't even to this day. I am so grateful that I had ingrained discipline into my days. *Discipline didn't just come along. Daily habits and simply just deciding to, even when I didn't want to, allowed discipline to become a part of me. Even to this day, I often don't 'want to,' but I do because I know discipline equals freedom in so many ways.*

For me it started with getting out of bed early, dating back to a teenager, to ride a couple of horses in training before school, continuing for years and then before work. And still to this day, I practice some form of physical commitment for myself, prior to my working day, even when it is the last thing, I feel like doing.

We are not always motivated, we are not always inspired, but we can always be disciplined. There is no excuse.

Isn't freedom what you really want? We all want freedom. I do and I know you do too. If you want to live and act with a sense of freedom then you must find a way to do things you don't necessarily want to do. To do what needs to be done, you must dig deep and find a way. Find a way to move toward the freedom you are yearning for.

Discipline is the only path to freedom.

Where can you discipline yourself in your life to find the freedom *within* your life?

Going to bed earlier?
Get out of bed earlier?
Go to the gym?

Exercise daily?
Begin that project?
Stop eating rubbish?
Eat vegetables and fruit daily?
Hydrate?

We all have days where we do not feel like doing it, whatever *it* may be, or sleeping in, struggling to get out of bed, or we will do it tomorrow, and before too long we have slowed down, lost the momentum, lost the drive, and over time life feels down, unfulfilled, and unhappy.

Within our home, we have over the last two decades now, often referred to the Nike logo, because it says it all.

We have said it out loud when one of us have been struggling, wavering, or if we have struggled to get our butt into gear. We have vocalised to get into the right mindset, with a no excuse attitude. **It has become a family mantra.**

"Nike. Just Do It."

When life comes along,
stand tall, stand proud.
Speak clearly.
Know when to listen.
Open your heart.
Connect with your heart.
Shine brightly,
Make a difference.

Food for Thought

You could live out your remaining days speaking in 'bumper stickers', and be the 'behind closed doors' rebel, silently nodding in agreement in the privacy of the cubicle in a public loo at the rebellious quote on the back of the door.

You could love like a Mills and Boone novel, or fist pump the air like a gold medallist athlete, and attempt to understand the 'fall to the knees' moment in complete gratitude, awe, and relief as a new world record holder. And, maybe briefly entertain the feeling of shattered disbelief, in the loss of missing the mark, falling to your knees this time, as your heart and guts are ripped out of you.

You can imagine what it would feel like, momentarily feeling another's triumph or pain. But *only* imagine.

Food for thought................

Rather than living off the back of another's wisdom, another's words, another's loss, another's victory, another's vision, another's world, and insights, wouldn't you rather rise, stand on your own two feet, with your own thinking process and point of view, within your own melancholy, heartbreaking, torn apart trauma, *and* healed pieces, in your own life?

Allow the quotes that YOU have discovered, the words which have come to YOU through YOUR own experience, pass your lips, so you may learn to talk your talk, then walk your walk.

Nothing wrong with appreciating the bumper sticker, light bulb moment, or having another's quote on your fridge or mirror, but what if you endeavoured to, as life passes through you, discover your own?

What if you **are** the rebel? The natural rebel who *has* nodded in agreement to a quote on the back of a public toilet door? Don't just nod in the privacy of a cubicle, go out and *be* the awakened rebel, teach by example, lead by example.

What if you are a healer? A poet? A creator? Then heal, rhyme, and create.

Love is not a Mills and Boone novel, a predictive format laid out before you. Life will not give that to you. Perfection will not find you love, influence will not find you love, money will not find you love, neediness will not find you love, and figuring yourself out before you find someone will not assure love.

But honesty, non-attachment, curiosity, fun, open heartedness, and authenticity, may just bring the opportunity across your path, and sometimes an organic magic can happen when you are least expecting it.

You may miss the target in this life many times, and fall to your knees. Business, love, loss, failures, betrayal, tragedy, shattered dreams. In fact, we are all guaranteed to experience and live these at one point in time.

We will feel beaten up, manhandled, squashed, black and blue as we fall to our knees, again and again.

But ………… could you still push off with scraped hands, grazed knees,

bruised ego, wounded heart, and tattered wings,

and still rise?

Each time life comes along.

You Have Got to Give Up
Part of Yourself

I want you to give up something from long ago,
that past thought which haunts you today,
remember your past can be from ten minutes ago,
thought you could deny or out run it? It does not work that
way.

For what you are not willing to change,
will always happily stay,
life is hard enough to decipher,
why would you consciously choose to stay this way?

You have got to be willing to give up part of yourself,
the old, subservient, and frayed,
you have got to give up part of yourself,
so, your mind, and old stories you no longer obey.

This life is one hell of an experiment,
we can dive deep, reach high or stay,
but you have got to give up part of yourself,
if you ever want to live daily unafraid.

So, I ask you now, what are you willing to do?
To let go the bondage, fearful and betrayed?
Are you willing now to give up part of yourself?
It is time to be life's bride, and no longer the bridesmaid.

Now you have given up part of yourself,
have you noticed there is more time for play?
The moment you gave up part of yourself,
life once again moved through you, in the most miraculous
of ways.

www.ingramcontent.com/pod-product-compliance
Lightning Source LLC
Chambersburg PA
CBHW051417090426
42737CB00014B/2717